ARTISTS OF THE HARLEM RENAISSANCE

ZORA NEALE HURSTON

LARA ANTAL

Cavendish
Square

New York

Published in 2017 by Cavendish Square Publishing, LLC
243 5th Avenue, Suite 136, New York, NY 10016

Library of Congress Cataloging-in-Publication Data

Names: Antal, Lara, author.
Title: Zora Neale Hurston : author / Lara Antal.
Description: New York : Cavendish Square Publishing, 2017. | Series: Artists of the Harlem Renaissance | Includes bibliographical references and index.
Identifiers: LCCN 2015036264 | ISBN 9781502610386 (library bound)
ISBN 9781502610393 (ebook)
Subjects: LCSH: Hurston, Zora Neale–Juvenile literature. | Novelists, American–20th century–Biography–Juvenile literature. | African American novelists–Biography–Juvenile literature. | African American women–Southern States–Biography–Juvenile literature. Folklorists–United States–Biography–Juvenile literature.
Classification: LCC PS3515.U789 Z6215 2016 | DDC 813/.52–dc23
LC record available at http://lccn.loc.gov/2015036264

Editorial Director: David McNamara
Editor: Elizabeth Schmermund
Copy Editor: Nathan Heidelberger
Art Director: Jeffrey Talbot
Designer: Stephanie Flecha
Production Assistant: Karol Szymcczuk
Photo Research: J8 Media

Printed in the United States of America

TABLE OF CONTENTS

PART 1

The Life of Zora Neale Hurston

"I mean to live and die by my own mind."

—*Zora Neale Hurston*

Opposite: Zora Neale Hurston was an author, researcher, and charismatic personality.

ALA. 44-NOTA.v 1-2   HABS

16-537

CHAPTER ONE

GROWING

Zora Neale Hurston was above all other things a storyteller. Inquisitive and smart, she was constantly exploring the world around her. However, what set her apart from other researchers was that Hurston took the essence of the things she learned and then recombined them into her own narratives. From a young dreaming girl, to writer in the **Harlem Renaissance**, to world traveler, no one could deny that Hurston had lived a life written by her own hand.

A NATURAL BORN STORYTELLER

Zora Neale Hurston was born on January 7, 1891, or at least, this is the date most historians agree upon. She was a natural storyteller and even wove stories into her own life: depending on the situation, Hurston would claim she was born anywhere between the 1890s to the early 1900s. Born in Notasulga, Alabama, as the fifth of eight children, Hurston moved with her family to

Opposite: Notasulga, Alabama—the birthplace of Zora Neale Hurston.

Eatonville, Florida, when she was only three years old. She would consider Eatonville her hometown, partly because she did not remember Alabama, but more importantly because it permanently shaped her outlook on life.

Eatonville, Florida

Eatonville was one of the first self-governing, all-black municipalities in the United States. Hurston described it as a completely "negro town": run by black folks, for black folks. Formed only ten years after **Reconstruction**, or the time period following the Civil War in which the federal government sought to rebuild and unify the United States, Eatonville embodied a new era of self-governance for black communities. A unique place, it drew over six thousand black residents, who arrived within three years of incorporation. The only white people who visited were travelers on their way to Orlando or physicians. In an all-black town, no one feared being treated as a second-class citizen: black residents could manage their own city on their own terms. The Hurstons saw the value and opportunity of such a place and in 1894 arrived at their new home.

The Hurston Family

John Hurston, Zora's father, was a large, muscular man who worked as a carpenter and zealous Baptist preacher. He gave dramatic sermons and calls to action in public and lost his temper at home. His showmanship even funneled into politics when, in 1887, he was elected as mayor of Eatonville. In 1902, John would become the head reverend at the largest church in town, Macedonia Missionary Baptist. Zora's mother, Lucy Potts Hurston, was far more reserved. She had a small, delicate frame and an even temperament. Lucy had worked as a schoolteacher and was very bright. She did not waste words and used her intellect for important matters. John often sought advice from his wife when navigating more precarious situations, while she in turn relied on her husband to take charge when a commanding presence was needed.

Zora was often compared to her older sister Sarah, who was feminine, quiet, and well behaved. Zora, on the other hand, was full of energy, imaginative, and sassy. She played outside with her brothers and got into trouble, concocted crazy stories about the world, and dreamed of adventures she might one day have. Zora's brash, confident personality did not always agree with her father's. John Hurston adored Sarah: she was the apple of his eye,

A historic home in modern-day Eatonville.

and he showered her with gifts and praise. Zora, however, gave him a huge headache. The two quarreled about this and that, and John scolded her for her rambunctious behavior.

Luckily for Zora, her mother, Lucy, always defended and supported her fiery spirit. According to Zora, Lucy told her children to "'jump at de sun.' We might not land on the sun, but at least we would get off the ground." These encouraging words, and her mother's love and guidance, would stick with Zora throughout her life.

The family lived in an eight-room house on 5 acres (2 hectares) of land. Though they were not wealthy, they lived well. The family never went hungry; between the fruit in their garden, the fish in the lakes, and the farm chickens, they always had food on the table. Biographer Robert Hemenway remarked that the family had "so many laying hens that the children sometimes boiled eggs in an iron kettle, then lay in the yard and ate until they were full."

Setting for a Story

Eatonville would be a constant source of inspiration for Hurston and would be featured as the setting in many of her stories. She described it as a city of "five lakes, three croquet courts, three hundred brown skins, three hundred good swimmers, plenty guavas, two schools, and no jail house." It wasn't just the buildings or the roads that captured Hurston's imagination: it was the people.

As a child, Hurston lingered whenever asked to go to the General Store. Owned by Joe Clarke, the founder of Eatonville, the store was a social hotspot. People gathered on the front porch for what Hurston called "lying sessions." Hemenway described these sessions as "constant verbal rituals contributing order, beauty, and poetry to the community's life." From stories, to playful competitions, to songs, these congregations filled young Zora's mind with literary **fodder**, or material, for years to come.

The townsfolk told tales that incorporated folk stories, biblical narratives, and other colloquial influences. Many of these stories were passed down through generations of oral tradition, dating back to pre-slavery, African origins. Some involved reoccurring characters, like Brer Rabbit, Sis Cat, Brer Bear, and Brer Fox. These **anthropomorphic** animals were **archetypes** for people who existed in the world of man: the tricky, gullible, wise, and naïve. Characters from the Bible, even God and the Devil, also played a part in these fun and instructive tales. All that existed in the world was fair game to heighten the drama or point out the humor and follies inherit in human nature.

Sometimes these tales got personal. Without malicious intent, the storytellers on Joe Clarke's porch would try to "out-do" one another by telling a more exciting story than the other. They exaggerated their plots and tweaked them to fit their own style.

Hurston would return to Eatonville many times in her adult life. Here she is with author Rochelle French and blues musician Gabriel Brown.

Biographer Janelle Yates describes this tit-for-tat: "Instead of calling somebody 'ugly', a talker would accuse him of being, 'so ugly they had to spread a sheet over his head at night so sleep could slip up on him.' Then they'd all laugh and think up something else."

Then, just as organically as stories emerged, so did music. Guitars, voices, and impromptu drums would break out in melodies and rhythms that lasted for minutes or hours.

Joe Clark's shop wasn't just the epicenter of frivolity, but the "heart and spring of the town." To Hurston, it represented the warmest and fondest aspects of black culture: community, expression, and imagination. It was in places like these that people explored, "through their mouths," the mysteries of this "world and the next one."

Imagination

When Hurston wasn't running errands to the store or doing chores around the house, she was out in the fresh air, dreaming up stories. Hemenway describes her magical world:

> When she played in the moonlight, Zora was convinced that the moon followed her, specially shining on his special child. She liked to climb to the top of one of the huge chinaberry trees which guarded the front gate and search the horizon; she wanted to see what the end of the world was like: "My shoes had sky-blue bottoms to them, and I was riding off to look at the belly-band of the world."

Most of all, Hurston like to sit on the gatepost and watch the world. From this viewpoint, she could watch travelers on their way to and from Orlando. She saw all kinds of people go by, and she longed to have an adventure of her own. In her essay "How It Feels to Be Colored Me," she describes how she communicated, and even traveled a little way, with these passersby:

My favorite place was atop the gatepost … Not only did I enjoy the show, but I didn't mind the actors knowing that I liked it. I usually spoke to them in passing. I'd wave at them and when they returned my salute, I would say something like this: "Howdy-do-well-I-thank-you-where-you-goin'?" Usually automobile or the horse paused at this, and after a queer exchange of compliments, I would probably "go a piece of the way" with them, as we say in farthest Florida. If one of my family happened to come to the front in time to see me, of course negotiations would be rudely broken off. But even so, it is clear that I was the first "welcome-to-our-state" Floridian, and I hope the Miami Chamber of Commerce will please take notice.

A Love of Learning

Zora's mother, Lucy, had instilled a love of learning in her children. An intelligent woman, Lucy had been a country schoolteacher in Alabama and now worked as a Sunday school teacher in Eatonville. Every night she gathered her eight children together to conduct lessons. She taught them long division and "parsing sentences in grammar." When the older children surpassed her knowledge, she continued to supervise the lessons, helping the younger ones focus and learning new things herself.

Zora was especially bright and had learned to read before she entered school. While in the fifth grade, a pair of "Yankee," or Northern, schoolteachers visited Zora's class. Zora volunteered to read aloud and gave a flawless rendition of the classical Greek tale of Pluto and Persephone. The teachers were so stunned by her performance that they invited her to visit with them. The women gave her sweet treats, pennies, and books. Zora had read through everything at school and had only a Bible at home. With this new gift, she was able to explore a whole new universe: from Grimm's fairy tales, Greek and Roman myths, and Norse

SQUARE-TOED DEATH

On more than one occasion Hurston would refer to the entity of Death as "square-toed," meaning it was formal in its actions and without leniency. The facts of death have not changed, but the way we deal with it has. At the turn of the century, southern African-American and Creole communities believed in **superstitions** as a means to reconcile their fear of death and the unknown. The first step toward deciphering the mystery of death was to anticipate it. There were omens, or prophetic signs or events, believed to herald death's arrival: a dog barking at 2 or 3 a.m., a rooster that flaps its wings backwards, or the sound of a woodpecker pecking in the neighborhood. If a full, green tree suddenly loses all its leaves, it means someone young is going to die. In addition to predicting death, many believed there were practices that could spare the living from the wrath of the dead. At funerals it was common to touch the deceased so as to avoid being haunted by their spirit. If the person held malice toward you in life, you should stick a pin into their body—this would prevent them from causing you harm from beyond the grave. When passing a graveyard, it was best not to look, otherwise you might see a ghost looking back. Though innocuous now, these beliefs gave people a sense of control when dealing with the merciless ways of death.

legends, to Rudyard Kipling and Robert Louis Steveson. The two schoolteachers returned north but continued to send her gifts, fueling Zora's thirst for knowledge.

WANDERINGS

Zora would soon face the end of one phase in her life, specifically, the end of her **idyllic** childhood. This would start her "wanderings … not so much in geography, but in time. Then not so much in time as in spirit."

The Death of Lucy Hurston

Lucy Hurston had been growing weaker from some time. Zora recalled her mother "kept getting thinner and thinner and her chest cold never got any better." This didn't worry the family at first because Lucy was, by nature, a frail woman. However, after she returned from Alabama to visit her dying sister, Lucy fell ill herself.

One day, Zora's mother told her daughter, "You know we all got to die one day and my day will be coming," and asked Zora to fulfill her dying wishes. Contrary to village custom, Lucy did not want the pillow taken from underneath her head, which was said to ease the suffering of the dying. She also did not want to cover the mirror or the clocks as local superstition dictated. They believed that reflective surfaces and time-telling devices could trap a spirit at the time of its death, imprisoning it to forever haunt the living.

Lucy's death was extremely traumatic for thirteen-year-old Zora. When she noticed a crowd gathering at home, she pushed her way into her mother's bedroom. Her mother was writhing in pain, and people began to remove her pillow and cover the mirrors and clocks. To their surprise, Zora violently protested, trying to express to her father her mother's dying wishes. John Hurston did not take heed, physically holding Zora down. After hours of agonizing pain, Lucy Hurston died. Zora wrote,

"Death had stirred from his platform in his secret place in our yard, and came into the house."

Zora would feel guilty for not fulfilling her mother's wishes. She blamed her father and the superstitious people of Eatonville, but mostly she blamed herself. She said, "If there is any consciousness after death, I hope that Mama knows I did my best. She must know how I have suffered for my failure."

Jacksonville

The next day, Lucy Hurston was buried. Though the family did not know, this was the last time they would all be together. Zora's siblings Bob and Sarah went back to their Baptist boarding school in Jacksonville. John Hurston threw himself into preaching and was rarely home. Zora was then sent to the same boarding school as her siblings. Within two weeks after her mother's death, Zora hopped on a train to Jacksonville.

Zora was lonely at school and found it hard to make friends because of her age. She rarely saw her older siblings on campus. When her sister Sarah stated she was feeling lonely, their father brought her home. Zora, however, had to stay. She tried to do her best: she won the regional spelling bee, excelled in her studies, and charmed her teachers. Things were starting to feel normal when she received a letter that said her father had remarried. It has been rumored that John Hurston's second wife, Mattie Moge, had been his mistress while Lucy was still alive. This new stepmother also had kicked Sarah, John Hurston's favorite, out of the house. Then Zora's father stopped paying Zora's school tuition; she was constantly being pulled aside by administrators and asked to pay her outstanding bill. When they realized she was helpless, they had her earn her keep by cleaning or doing chores around campus. The school year was coming to an end and Zora couldn't wait for her father to take her home.

However, instead of meeting with her father, the school's director pulled Zora aside to give her another letter: John wasn't coming, and he wanted the school to adopt her. Taking pity on Zora, the director handed her a dollar and a half as fare to get her home, to be repaid by her father once she arrived. The next day, Zora boarded a steamboat down the St. John's River to Sanford, then caught a train to Maitland.

The Feather Mattress

John's new wife felt no love for his children: when Zora arrived, her siblings had already been badgered until they left. Mattie Hurston also took to using all of Lucy's old belongings. It was her disregard for a feather mattress from Zora's grandfather that proved too much. In less than a week, Zora retaliated: she grabbed the mattress and dragged it out of the house. John and Mattie threatened to hurt Zora if she didn't stop. Her father pulled out a knife, and if it hadn't been for the intervention of Zora's brother John, he might have used it. Scared and saddened, Zora left the Hurston home with her brother and mattress in hand.

Nowhere but the Road

Hurston had nowhere to go. She was shuffled between relatives, each one tiring of her and sending her off. She tried to work to earn her keep but couldn't keep a job because of her sharp tongue. Having grown up in a supportive, all-black community, Hurston had never encountered racism or **classism** before. Suddenly, while working menial jobs for white employers, she was being treated differently. For the first time, Hurston felt what it was like to be a "little colored girl." She refused to act **ingratiatingly**, or in a manner to gain approval, just because they expected her to act in this way. She kept her dignity but at the expense of her pocketbook: for the first time, Hurston knew real poverty. She later wrote that it was through poverty that "people could be slave ships in shoes."

Finally, Hurston caught a break: a young singer named Miss M was looking for a maid to help on tour with a theater group.

During the interview, Hurston lied about her age, saying she was twenty years old, but Miss M could see this wasn't true. However, she liked Hurston's confidence and hired her on the spot. Just like that, Hurston began traveling like she had always dreamed.

Hurston was the only black and Southern person in the famous Gilbert and Sullivan troupe: most of these actors had never heard the colloquial phrases and clever insults she used, gleaned from Joe Clarke's shop. Regardless, Hurston felt at home. Members of the troupe bought her sweet treats and sodas, sang songs to her, and told her stories about the world. As Hemenway describes, working and living with the troupe was the "major educational experience of her youth, liberating her from the **provincialism** she had known all her life." She was enthralled by the possibilities that lay beyond central Florida. After eighteen fun months, Hurston said goodbye to her friends and headed to Baltimore, determined to finish school and see the world on her own terms.

EDUCATION

In September 1917, Hurston enrolled in Morgan College, the high school division of Morgan State University. This was an all-black school attended by mainly middle- and upper-class families. Hurston was a poor girl who owned only "one dress, a change of underwear, and a pair of tan oxfords." However, her raw intelligence and determination kept her competitive with her peers. She worked various jobs during the day and attended classes at night. Her sporadic education had left her with a lot of catching up to do, but she soon received credit for two years by exam and finished at Morgan College in 1918.

Howard University

Hurston's next ambition was to attend Howard University, which she called the "capstone of Negro education in the world." The largest black university in America, Howard was founded in

1867 in Washington, DC, with the goal of educating its students "intellectually, morally, [and] socially ... emphasizing what might be called a classical education." Its scholastic prowess was "for Negroes what Harvard was for Whites." It was also home to "Negro money, beauty, and prestige," assets Hurston felt she did not have. The odds were against her: in 1917, there were only 2,132 black students enrolled in the US.

Despite these facts, Hurston moved to Washington, DC, during the summer of 1918 to find a job and settle herself before the school year. She worked as a waitress at the Cosmos Club and saved up enough money to fund her first semester at Howard. Hurston was disappointed to find she didn't have enough credits to start her college career, so after a semester of preparatory classes, she officially earned her high school diploma in May 1919 and began taking college-level courses the following fall.

Howard University's campus in Washington, DC.

Balancing School and Work

Biographer Valerie Boyd describes how Hurston was moved by the music and the swell of students and teachers at her first school assembly, whispering to the spirit of Howard Univerity: "You have taken me in. I am a tiny bit of your greatness. I swear you you that I shall never make you ashamed of me."

Though Hurston was excited, her first semester grades were unremarkable. This might have been due to her rigorous schedule: unlike many of her peers, Hurston had to balance school life with work. She took odd jobs as a waitress or a maid for Washington's wealthiest black families.

Her main source of income, however, came from working as a manicurist. The barbershop she worked at was located in downtown Washington, DC, and served white clientele only. The entrepreneur behind this business was a black man named George Robinson. "He had no education himself," Hurston wrote, "but was for it. He would give any Howard University student a job if they could qualify, even if it was only for a few hours a week." This is what Hurston did, working from 3:30 to 8:30 p.m. every afternoon, allowing her time for classes and study. Due to the shop's central location, Hurston's clients were often white men of power: bankers, journalists, lawmakers, and politicians. They felt comfortable discussing everything with her because, as a black female, her discretion did not matter. "I would learn things from holding the hands of men like that," Hurston said, referring not only to gossip, but to the fact that these white men were similar to the black men she knew: in some ways, their stories resembled those told on Joe Clark's shop porch.

Collegiate Life

After her first semester, Hurston began to improve academically. Due to her full schedule, she would complete a year and a half's worth of school between 1919 and 1924, receiving an associate's

Georgia Douglas Johnson hosted literary salons and discussions at her home in DC.

degree in 1920 and continuing to pursue a bachelor's degree thereafter. However, her time wasn't idle: Hurston took full advantage of collegiate life and the Washington, DC, literary scene. She joined Zeta Phi Beta, a new sorority for young black women, and she became a member of the "Howard Players," a theatrical group on campus. Most importantly, Hurston participated in groups whose focus was on the craft of writing. She spent many nights in "marathon literary discussions" with other students at the home of Georgia Douglas Johnson, a prominent black poet. In school, Hurston shone: her teachers praised her for her talent and wit. She garnered the attention of Alain Locke, a young philosophy professor and founder of Howard's literary club called Stylus. He encouraged Hurston to apply to the annual competition that determined the club's members. She was accepted and began to publish her first writings.

A Burgeoning Author

Hurston's first mentor would be Professor Alain Locke. Considered the "Dean" of the Harlem Renaissance, he was one of the most important American philosophers of the twentieth century. A Harvard graduate and the first African-American Rhodes Scholar, Locke came to Howard University in 1912. For many years he would play a pivotal role in Hurston's literary career.

Hurston published her first pieces in the literary club's publication *Stylus* in the May 1921 issue. Included was a poem entitled "O Night," and the story "John Redding Goes to Sea." While her poem was well received, it was "John Redding" that stood out. Taking place in a fictionalized Eatonville, the plot is a classic tragedy that uses rural characters and strong southern dialects. No one had ever read a story that utilized the colloquial elements of black culture for literary **allegories**, and it made an impression. Hurston was attempting to make art out of her own life experiences, as biographer Boyd describes: "Despite any amateurish flaws, 'John Redding Goes to Sea' illustrates that Hurston was on the verge of an epiphany: she had begun to realize that the lives—and the language—of ordinary black country folk had enormous literary potential."

In 1922, Hurston published three poems in *Negro World*, the Universal Negro Improvement Association's (UNIA) magazine. This would be the first and last time she published her poetry nationally. In 1923, she published a few humorous essays in Howard University's yearbook, as well as a quote and personal motto. Her ambition was to "establish herself in Greenwich Village where she may write stories and poems and live an unrestrained Bohemian," and her personal saying was, "I have a heart with room for every joy." These sentiments foreshadowed the next step in her life: moving to New York.

CHAPTER TWO

EXPRESSION

The Harlem Renaissance, or the New Negro Movement as it was known at the time, was a creative and social movement that took place in the neighborhood of Harlem, New York. From the end of World War I to the mid-thirties, Harlem was home to some of the greatest musicians, performers, philosophers, writers, poets, political thinkers, and artists of the black community. Alain Locke coined the term the "New Negro," to describe this new wave of black intellectuals and artists. The "New Negro" was well rounded, educated, and inventive, and opposed derogatory depictions of the "old negro." The art of the Harlem Renaissance became the vibrant expression of this newfound self-autonomy and pride in black culture. Locke felt Hurston's talent could add to the cultural climate in New York City. Although he "rarely saw promise in young women," Locke prized Hurston not only for her intelligence, but for her humble and rural beginnings. Historian Steven Watson noted that Hurston "could provide the connection to the black folk heritage that Locke considered essential to the creation of a New Negro literature."

Opposite: This intersection runs through the heart of Harlem.

Opportunity magazine published many young writers of the Harlem Renaissance.

Opportunity Magazine

In the fall of 1924, Locke recommended Hurston to Charles Johnson. Johnson was the editor and founder of *Opportunity: A Journal of Negro Life*, which was the official publication of the Urban League, an advocacy organization for African Americans. A sociologist who would later become the first African-American president of Fisk University, Johnson was searching for literary voices that could define the "New Negro" movement. The magazine held open contests to find new authors and invited the winners to attend awards dinners in New York City. Here they could meet with other intellectuals and editors to further their own careers, all while strengthening the artistic merit of black work. Johnson read "John Redding Goes to Sea" and encouraged Hurston to submit other stories to *Opportunity*. Eagerly, she sent him the story "Drenched in Light," which was then published in the 1924 December issue of the magazine.

Hurston's story was heralded as a success, and the following year she submitted two more works to *Opportunity*. The first story, "Spunk," took place in another fictional Eatonville, and the second, *Color Struck*, was a play that depicted Florida folk life. Both stories won second place in the *Oppportunity* contest and earned Hurston an invitation to the contest awards dinner.

This was her first foray into the literary world, where she found herself "honored as one of the prominent talents in the new movements in the black arts."

Barnard

At one of these *Opportunity* dinners, Hurston met Annie Nathan Meyer. Meyer was a well-known novelist and advocate for women's education. She also founded Barnard Women's College in response to Columbia University's refusal to admit women. The two began chatting, and by the end of the evening, Meyer had offered Hurston a full scholarship to Barnard. Hurston immediately accepted— she could continue her education at one of the nation's most respected schools and do so with no financial burden to herself. In spring 1925, she moved to New York City and transferred to Barnard College for the fall. In a letter addressed to Meyer on May 12, 1925, Hurston described her excitement and gratitude for this change: "I am tremendously encouraged now. My typewriter is clicking away till all hours of the night. I am striving desperately for a toe-hold on the world. You see, your interest keys me up wonderfully—I must not let you be disappointed in me."

Living in New York

Though Hurston's tuition was covered, she still needed to pay for living expenses. At another *Opportunity* dinner, Hurston found her next employer, Fannie Hurst, who hired her as a secretary. Unfortunately

A Harlem street, circa 1925

Harlem was an exciting place to be, full of art and nightlife. Here is a dance club, circa 1927.

for both women, Hurston was not suited for the profession: her shorthand was illegible and her filing was "a game of find the thimble." However, Hurst kept Hurston on as a chauffer and companion, and the two formed a strong bond. Hurst said she was often taken aback by how Hurston could "race ahead of my thoughts and interject with an impatient suggestion or clarification of what I wanted to say."

During her first year in New York, Hurston lived in six different residences, eventually settling in Harlem. This was indicative of her larger feeling toward life: Hurston wanted to experience it all. From uptown to downtown, lowbrow to highbrow, black folks and white folks, she wanted to engage and learn from everyone. As Hemenway describes, Hurston worked her life from all angles:

BEING COLORED ME

When Hurston arrived at Barnard in the fall of 1925, she was the college's only black student and, thus, occupied an interesting social position. Her essay "How It Feels to Be Colored Me" describes her sense of "otherness":

> I feel most colored when I am thrown against a sharp white background. For instance at Barnard. "Beside the waters of the Hudson" I feel my race. Among the thousand white persons, I am a dark rock surged upon, and overswept, but through it all, I remain myself. When covered by the waters, I am; and the ebb but reveals me again.

Being black often made her feel special. She wrote to Meyer that "the girls at Barnard are perfectly wonderful to me. They literally drag me to the teas on Wednesday and then behave as if I'm the guest of honor—so eager are they to assure me that I am desired there." Hurston's popularity was undoubtedly due to the combination of her humorous personality, race, and close ties with the famous Fannie Hurst. When speaking to her black friends, she often bragged about her ability to mix favorably with people of many ethnicities, and was even quoted saying, "In fact I am received so well that if someone would come along and try to turn me white I'd be quite peevish at them."

She could walk into a room of strangers, whether on Park Avenue or at a Harlem rent party, and almost immediately gather people, charm, amuse, and impress them, until it did not seem at all unnatural to be offering her whatever she might want. She was a perfect mimic, and displayed a wide range of storytelling techniques learned form the masters of Joe Clarke's store porch … She could be tart, referring to racial uplifters as "**Negrotarians**," but she sometimes spent hours of a busy schedule reassuring a depressed fellow artist; her apartment was always open to someone needing a place to stay.

WRITING IN THE RENAISSANCE

Hurston spent only two paragraphs in her autobiography, *Dust Tracks on a Road*, on the Harlem Renaissance. Despite the fact that she didn't speak often about her role in the Renaissance, she was well known to other artists in Harlem at the time. Langston Hughes described her as "certainly the most amusing" of artists and "full of side-splitting anecdotes, humorous takes and tragic-comic stories." In addition to her larger-than-life personality, Hurston added to the literary wealth of the movement. Her 1926 story "Muttsy" won second place in *Opportunity*, "Possum or Pig" was published in *Forum*, and "The Eatonville Anthology," appeared in the *Messenger* magazine. However it was her contribution to Alain Locke's 1925 seminal anthology, *The New Negro*, that secured her place as a contributor to the Renaissance. As the unofficial manifesto of the movement, the volume contained poetry, essays, and fiction, including Hurston's previously published story "Spunk." Locke wrote in the introduction that these works represented the "spiritual coming of age" for black Americans as evidenced by the "unusual burst of creative expression" coming from these young creators.

Once labeled as an important black creator, Hurston was able to meet with other like-minded artists and find patrons for

Getting Religion by Archibald John Motley Jr. While Motley never lived in Harlem, his paintings capture the spirit of the "New Negro Movement" as it developed in cities like New Orleans and Chicago.

her work. However, sometimes it felt strange to be exhibited in such a way. Arna Bontemps, another young novelist and poet, remembered what it felt like to be considered "significant":

> When we were not too busy having fun, we were shown off and exhibited and presented in scores of places to all kinds of people. And we heard the sighs of wonder, amazement, and sometimes admiration when it was whispered or announced that here was one of the "New Negros."

Hurston was not bothered by the attention, but she was concerned with Locke's manifesto for the New Negro movement. He felt artists should use their heritage not just "purely for the sake of art" but as a means to elevate the race's social standing in

America. Locke emphasized young creators because the cultural recognition they earned would "prove the key to the revaluation of the Negro which must precede or accompany any considerable further betterment of race relations." However, Hurston did not want her work to represent the entire black race but to be seen as an expression of her own unique vision. Many artists felt similarly, asserting that while being black was essential to their work, it wasn't the punch line. It was this struggle, to find an identity that could embrace black heritage without being pigeonholed by it, that pushed the new artists of the Harlem Renaissance toward their own systems of expression.

Fire!!

Hurston had met author Langston Hughes at the *Opportunity* awards dinner in May 1925. Hughes was one of the most important authors of the Harlem Renaissance. Referred to as the "people's

This photograph of a Harlem couple, taken by artist James Van Der Zee, is a beautiful testament to the emerging black middle and upper classes of the 1920s.

poet," Hughes focused his writings on sorrows and joys of black life in America. He rejected the ideas of the Renaissance's **genteel** thinkers, like Alain Locke and W. E. B. Du Bois, because they conformed to white, **Eurocentric** ideals as a means to achieve racial equality. Hughes and his peers didn't want to give up the richness of black culture but instead celebrate its range: from the intellectual to the folkloric, every aspect was a source of pride.

In the summer of 1926, the magazine *Fire!!: Devoted to Younger Negro Artists* was published by a group of artists who called themselves the "Nigeratti," a term meant to shock the stuffier intellectuals of Harlem. Hurston, Hughes, author Wallace Thurman, and writer and painter Bruce Nugent were at the center of the group, but there were many famous satellite participants who were poets, columnists, artists, actors, and musicians. Each week they met to discuss literature, politics, and gossip, as well as to party. As Hemenway describes, the "festivities were raucous, with brilliant talk, and as the evenings wore on, outrageous good times." Hurston, calling herself the "Queen of the Nigeratti," often hosted for her newfound Bohemian family. Hemenway describes:

> Her apartment was always open for Niggerati meetings, with a pot on the stove that visitors were expected to contribute to in order to create a common stew. At other times she fired okra, or cooked Florida eel. Zora had moved into the apartment without furniture or money; yet within a few days it had been completely furnished by her friends with everything from decorative silver birds … to a footstool for the living room. To celebrate, she gave a "hand chicken dinner," so called, Hughs claimed, because she forgot to ask for forks.

This natural energy funneled into *Fire!!* While Locke's and Du Bois's *The New Negro* could be seen as "a subtly designed piece of propaganda … serving the ideal of Justice for the New Negro in American life," *Fire!!* operated on more aggressive terms. It laid bare the group's "esthetic frustration ... with the appropriation of their talents by the racial propagandists." For its first issue, Hurston reworked and republished her play *Color Struck* and included a new story called "Sweat." Considered one of her best short stories, Hemenway describes its brillance:

> ["Sweat"] builds a tragic structure around a washerwoman and her unemployed husband, dignifying her labor and his insecurity, making them victims of both their individual inadequacies and their larger fate. A perfect fusing of the Eatonville environment and the high seriousness of self-conscious literature, it illustrates the unlimited potential in Hurston's folk material.

Eatonville inspired Hurston's fiction and anthropological work.

Despite Hurston's contribution, the magazine failed after one volume. Edited, printed, and paid for by the artists, there were financial and organizational issues from the beginning. Bad public reception and a few strokes of bad luck (ironically, a fire destroyed several hundred copies) sealed the publication's fate. History would agree with Hurston when she said, "I suppose that 'Fire' has gone to ashes quite, but I still think the idea is good."

SPYGLASS OF ANTHROPOLOGY

Throughout 1925 and 1926, Hurston saw herself as an artist and contributer to the Harlem Renaissance. But, by 1927, she became less interested in writing because of her new passion: **anthropology**. Hurston switched her major and began studying under the tutelage of professor Franz Boas. Hurston deeply respected the professor. He challenged her intellectually, and as Boyd notes, Hurston "hung on Boas's every word." She assisted Boas for two summers while in school, measuring the heads of African Americans in Harlem for a study he was conducting. Hurston lovingly refer to him as "Papa Franz," and as Boyd remarks, "years later, as a mature artist and scholar, she still would regard Boas as 'The King of Kings.'"

Anthropology became Hurston's major inspiration as an author and scholar. She had always felt that her "parents and their neighbors perpetuated a rich oral literature without self-consciousness." She knew that Eurocentric culture seldom recognized this type of creativity and that when it was acknowledged it was often misunderstood. Suddenly, with anthropology, Hurston could gather scientific "facts" about the lifestyles, heritage, and beliefs of her people and present them to an eager audience. As Hemenway describes, "she acquired the relatively rare opportunity to confront her culture both emotionally and analytically, both as subject and object." Hurston explained:

I couldn't see it [culture] for wearing it. It was only when I was off in college, away from my native surroundings that I could see myself like somebody else and stand off and look at my garment. Then I had the spyglass of Anthropology to look through at that.

Fieldwork

In February 1927, Boas gave Hurston some good news: he had secured funds from two foundations for her to conduct fieldwork in the South. She would have a total $1,400 to use for six months of fieldwork. When Boas asked her where she'd like to go, she immediately answered Florida. Not only did she have firsthand knowledge of the region, but Florida's diverse population would allow her to gather a "cross section of the Negro south in one state." Little research had been done about black culture in the South. Furthermore, no native southerner had ever conducted the research. In this way, Hurston felt she had a unique advantage.

Hurston returned to Eatonville that same month. She was happy to find the town hadn't changed much, and many of the townsfolk still remembered her. With her "spyglass" of anthropology to look through, she could see how unique Eatonville was. Boyd describes:

Self-governing and self-determining, [Eatonville] was markedly different from the places where most of Zora's Harlem Renaissance colleagues had grown up ... [Their] lifelong exposure to white interference and disapproval had taken a psychological toll that Zora could hardly imagine. Now, more than ever, she realized that all-black Eatonville was largely untrammeled by racism and its debilitating effects. It was a place (rare in America, Zora now knew) where black people were free from any indoctrination and inferiority.

However, Hurston found it difficult to step away from familiar faces and be solely a scientist. She had other difficulties, as well: her interviews revealed stories she already knew, and some townsfolk were confused and apprehensive about her motives.

This was the beginning of an unsuccessful tour of the South. While southern at heart, Hurston appeared like a polished northerner, an outsider. In addition, she had trouble scientifically and systematically observing the conversation rather than taking part in it. As Boyd describes, this was a big change for Hurston, who "had been the life of every party she'd attended in Harlem [but] was now required to be a conscientious wallflower." It was also dangerous to travel alone in the South as a black woman. She had heard many stories of rape, robbery, and lynching, and most hotels were strictly segregated. Often "Sassy Sussie," her aptly named car, was her spot for a good night's sleep.

Detours

One of the only highlights of this time spent in Eatonville was that Hurston was able to reconnect with her brother Bob and her other siblings. Though she learned of the sad news of her father's death, her visit with her siblings was otherwise positive. Hurston described: "I felt the warm embrace of kin and kind for the first time since the night after my mother's funeral."

During this time, and much to her own amazement, Hurston married her longtime lover Herbert Sheen. The two initially met at Howard University but separated when Sheen moved, though they kept in contact through letters. Now a Chicago doctor, Sheen drove down to St. Augustine, Florida, and asked for Hurston's hand in marriage after five years of separation. However, both parties soon realized their marriage would not work with their careers: Hurston did not want to be a physician's wife, and Sheen said he had no interest in "tramping around and finding the nitty-gritty part of folklore." She sent him back to Chicago, and the two would officially divorce in 1931, remaining good friends.

Langston Hughes
in 1954

Bonding with Hughes

After months of unsuccessful work in Florida, Hurston headed to Mobile, Alabama, to find Cudjo Lewis, believed to be the sole survivor of the last slave ship to the United States. Hurston interviewed him briefly but had difficulties with his heavy accent and reluctance toward newcomers. Afterward, she coincidently ran into Langston Hughes. They decided to travel north together, making pit stops to gather folk songs, tall tales, and explore remote towns and country churches. In Georgia, they visited the Toomer Plantation, met with turpentine farmers, and learned of hoodoo doctors. In the city of Macon, they saw the famous jazz singer Bessie Smith perform. She told them: "The trouble with white folks singing the blues is that they can't get low down enough." For two writers who highlighted folk tales and common experiences in their own work, this sentiment resonated. On the road back to New York, they discussed collaborating on a folk opera, using all that they had seen as material for their project.

When Hurston returned to New York, she had little to show for her trip. She wrote that, "considering [my mood] going south, I went back to New York with my heart beneath my knees in some lonesome valley." Boas, too, was let down. However, she realized later that he was "not as disappointed as he let me think. He knew I was green and feeling my oats, and that only bitter disappointment was going to purge me. It did." With a helpful dose of humility, Hurston threw herself into anthropology once more.

Godmother

In September 1927, Hurston met Charlotte Mason. A wealthy widow in her seventies, Mason was what Hurston called a Negrotarian, an upper-class, white liberal who financially supported black artists. Mason was probably the most extensive patron of the Renaissance: she paid Alain Locke handsomely for his on-demand consultations, covered all of Langston Hughes's living expenses, and supported a host of other artists and researchers. It was estimated that during the late 1920s and 1930s, Mason gave between $50,000 to $75,000 to her protégés. She was motivated by her own philosophy, as Boyd describes:

> Mason believed in cosmic energies and intuitive powers ... sure that "primitive" people, particularly American Indians and Negroes, were innately more in tune with these supernatural forces than were whites, who, in Mason's view, were not only overly civilized but spiritually barren.

Mason had once been an amateur anthropologist, spending time with Native American tribes in the Great Plains. Hughes described her as "very old and white-haired, but amazingly modern in her ideas, in her knowledge of books and the theater, of Harlem, and of everything taking place in the world."

Mason instantly loved Hurston, and Hurston's intelligence and humility. As Boyd describes:

> Although she was thoroughly learned, Zora was unlike Locke and other carefully mannered Negroes of Mason's acquaintance in that her negritude seemed undiminished by her education. Zora's grammar was proper yet free from affectation. She did not pitch her voice in a way to mask the blackness of its timbre, nor did she shamefacedly chase the South out of her diction. Zora was, a delighted Mason observed, as *Negro* as she could be.

On December 8, 1927, Hurston was invited back to Mason's Park Avenue home to consider a proposition: she would receive full funding for a year-long research trip to the South to collect folklore, with the possibility of extending into 1929. The contract had stipulations: Hurston must keep the patron's identity a secret and refer to her as "Godmother." Unlike Mason's other "godchildren," Hurston was not asked to create her own work, but was hired on behalf of Mason herself. The contract clearly stated Mason was "desirous of obtaining and compiling certain data," but "unable … to undertake the collecting of this information in person." Hurston would be an employee and only allowed to send her findings to her employer. She could not publish or discuss anything with anyone. These rules did not bother Hurston, so she eagerly signed the contract. She received a stipend of $200 a month, a film camera, and an automobile (selling off "Sassy Sussie" for a Chevrolet.) On December 14, Hurston boarded a train south to begin researching southern folklore, this time to great success.

Second Chance

Hurston's first stop was Mobile, Alabama, to interview Cudjo Lewis again. She visited him for a month, taking notes and film footage, and eventually gained his trust. He spoke about his experience being stolen from his home in Nigeria and placed aboard the slave ship *Clotilde*. Hurston was moved by his pain, noting how "after seventy-five years he still had that tragic sense of loss. That yearning for blood and cultural ties. That sense of mutilation. It gave me something to feel about."

In early February, she traveled to Eatonville and then to Polk County, Florida, landing in the town of Loughman. Full of tough men and even tougher women, the Everglades Cypress Lumber Company employed most of the town and ran the local boarding house. Hurston took a room and tried to befriend the locals, but without luck. Soon they began to exchange pleasantries, but it was obvious they did not trust her.

Hurston described this paradox of surface-level friendliness as "feather-bed resistance," meaning that these African Americans evaded questions about themselves by being friendly, while the outsider was never the wiser. Hurston wrote, "we let the probe enter, but it never comes out. It gets smothered under a lot of laughter and pleasantries." Eventually she found the reason her efforts were being thwarted: her shiny new car had convinced everyone that she was a tax officer, detective, or law enforcer. In response, she concocted her own persona as a **bootlegger**, or someone who sold or made alcohol illegally, running from the law. This also explained her wealthy city clothes, which she soon traded in for modest frocks.

Hurston slowly gained the trust, and stories, of the people in Loughman. She met characters: from Mack Ford, one of the greatest storytellers, to Big Sweet, the toughest and most charming woman to embody the blues. Using the participant-observer technique, taught to her by Boas, she immersed herself in the culture: drinking moonshine, dancing at town gatherings, and even accompanying the workmen to the cypress swamp (an impressive feat in the male-dominated town.) She took excursions to nearby phosphate mines in Mulberry, Lakeland, and Peirce, where she "collected a bundle of children's tales and games." By the end of her time, she would have a rich collection of tales, which she began to organize into anthropological categories of her own design.

On February 29, 1928, Zora received her BA in anthropology and became the first black woman to graduate from Barnard. However, as Boyd describes, she could not have "been further away from Barnard's consecrated corridors. The thirty-seven-year-old graduate was deep in Florida answering the call of anthropology."

CHAPTER THREE

MASTERY

Though dedicated to anthropology, Hurston never divorced herself from the idea of being a creative writer. A conflict of interest for most, the two were inseparable for Hurston. She wrote to Hughes, "I am getting inside of Negro art and lore. I am beginning to see really ... this is going to be big. Most gorgeous possibilities are showing themselves constantly." Hurston sent many secret letters to Hughes, but few to Mason. Hughes encouraged her to send their godmother more, but Hurston was always careful to keep some research to herself, hoping to utilize it when she was no longer under contract.

Hurston's time at Loughman ended with a bang, or rather a slash. A local woman, Lucy, was jealous of Hurston and felt she had eyes for her ex-boyfriend, Slim. At a local dance Lucy pulled out a knife and headed toward Hurston, only to be headed off by Big Sweet, who had promised to protect Hurston. Then chaos ensued: "It seemed anybody who had any fighting to do decided

Opposite: Zora Neale Hurston in Belle Glade, Florida, circa 1935.

HOODOO

Hoodoo, conjure, obeah, rootwork, and voodoo are terms to describe a set of beliefs and practices in which a properly trained person can use magic to alter situations that seem otherwise impossible to fix. The word "vodou," which is the basis of both "hoodoo" and the Haitian religion "voodoo," derives from *vodu*, meaning "spirit" or "diety" in Fon, the language of present-day Benin, West Africa. The intensity of the faith can range from basic **sympathetic magic** to a full-blown religion. Seasoned practitioners of hoodoo are known as doctors and use their powers to help with issues like easing physical ailments, helping romantic relationships, encouraging favorable luck toward legal and business matters, and placing curses or hexes on enemies.

Defining hoodoo can be a difficult task because its practices change according to each practitioner: a root doctor could simply be a medicine man who prescribes the use of herbs and roots, or it could refer to a conjure man who uses natural ingredients for supernatural effects. Hoodoo's ancient traditions began in Africa but, due to the slave trade, fused with Caribbean, South American, Creole, and even Christian belief systems. Hoodoo still thrives today, as well as its offshoots like Candomblé and Santería, in areas of the southern United States.

to settle-up then and there. Switch-blades, ice-picks, and old fashioned razors were out … Curses, oaths, cries, and the whole place was in motion."

Hurston escaped, packed her things, and drove off. She wrote, "When the sun came up I was a hundred miles up the road, headed for New Orleans."

New Orleans

Between her time in Polk County and a short stop in Magazine, Alabama, Hurston had collected enough materials to publish an entire volume. She wrote, "I am getting much more material in a given area/space & time than before because I am learning better technique." However, she came to New Orleans in August 1928 for another reason: to expand her knowledge of hoodoo. Discovering hoodoo's true workings in New Orleans would not be an easy task. Hurston described its secrecy, and thus, effectiveness: "It is not the accepted theology of the Nation and so believers conceal their faith. Brother from sister, husband from wife. Nobody can say where it begins or ends. Mouths don't empty themselves unless the ears are sympathetic and knowing."

Hurston approached her research as she always had: by immersing herself in the culture. She sought out the most knowledgeable hoodoo doctors and apprenticed herself to them. With each master she submitted to a rigorous initiation process to prove her worthiness. These initiation rites ranged from the uncomfortable to the gruesome. This level of dedication proved she was both a serious scholar and a unique woman: it would be hard to imagine Hurston's more urbane colleagues taking on such challenges. By the end of her time in New Orleans, Hurston was the foremost expert on hoodoo in America. The trip affirmed her belief that, contrary to popular belief, the common people held immense power. She wrote, "The man in the gutter is the god-maker, the creator of everything that lasts."

Making Sense of It All

In April 1929, Mason extended her contract, and Hurston moved to Eau Gallie, Florida, to sort through over ninety-five thousand words of story material, information on children's games, conjuring and religious materials, photographs, and film. She wrote to Boas for help, asking if her ethnographic conclusions represented, "all the life and color of my people … [but left] no loop-holes for the scientific crowd to rend and tear." She sent some of her findings to an increasingly anxious Mason, but kept most of them to herself. When Hurston finished her first draft about lore and religion, she said, "I shall now set it aside to cool till it grows inside of me."

In August, Hurston headed to Miami to continue with her research, secretly writing skits and music for the folk opera with Hughes (against Godmother's explicit orders.) Though productive, Hurston felt a "little depressed spiritually." Then, while in the city, she stumbled upon a performance of Bahamian music and dance. She fell in love instantly: it stuck her as "more original, dynamic, and African" than anything she had seen before. So without notice to her patron, Hurston sailed to Nassau, the capital of the Bahamas, on September 12, 1929.

Bahamas

Hurston admired the Bahamas for its natural and cultural beauty. Everything was alive with music: residents told her, "You do anything, we put you in sing." She found many of the natives knew which African tribes they descended from and could speak dialects. Before the end of September, Hurston had collected twenty songs, recorded three reels of folk dances, including the "Fire Dance," and even learned how to "jump," or dance, in the traditional ways.

However, on September 28, a devastating five-day hurricane hit Nassau. With 150-mile-per-hour (240-kilometer-per-hour) gusts of winds, Hurston described it as "horrible in its intensity and duration." During the second night of the storm, she had

A post office in Eau Gallie, Florida, where Hurston conducted anthropological work.

a premonition and insisted that she and her housemates leave immediately. The building collapsed moments later, and Hurston, like so many other Bahamians, was rendered homeless. The following days, she scrounged for shelter and food, and witnessed the horrible sight of "dead people washing around on the streets when it was over."

DRAMA

Charlotte Mason had grown more controlling over Hurston. Godmother's letters were often erratic, racist, and indicated she no longer cared to support her African-American protégées. However, she changed her mind when she viewed Hurston's film footage. Eager for Hurston to write a folklore book, Mason sent her to Westfield, New Jersey, to work alongside Langston Hughes and typist Louise Thompson. Instead, Hurston and Hughes worked on *Mule Bone: A Comedy of Negro Life*, their long discussed folk play, while Thompson transcribed their ideas. Since the project was made without their patron's consent, Thompson wasn't being paid for her work. Hughes suggested splitting authorship and future profits three ways, but Hurston strongly protested, suggesting they pay her out of pocket. When Hurston asked her, Thompson said she didn't want anything. Hurston suspected Hughes had secretly made bigger promises to the typist. Suspicious about the pair's intentions and feeling outnumbered, Hurston left Westfield.

A month later, Charlotte Mason cut off Hughes's funding. Distraught and broke, he turned to the *Mule Bone* script. He desperately tried to reconnect, but Hurston was still upset by his betrayal. She had rewritten the script, removing Hughes's contributions. In January 1931, while in Cleveland, Ohio, Hughes heard a production of *Mule Bone* was being performed. This shocked Hurston, too—their mutual friend Carl Van Vechten had passed an earlier draft to a director who thought it was ready to be performed. Though a misunderstanding, the damage had been done: the two were embroiled in an aggressive exchange of letters, lawyer consultations, and copyright filings. In a last effort to reconcile, Hughes and Hurston flew to Cleveland to approve the performance. However, Hurston canceled the operation when she discovered Hughes had brought Thompson to testify against her in court. Hurston claimed full ownership over *Mule Bone*, but their friendship and creative collaboration would never be restored.

Adaptations

Hurston wrote several skits for a **revue**, or a light theatrical performance comprised of skits, songs, dances, and satirical scenes, called *Fast and Furious*. Supposedly a depiction of African-American life, the performance was seen as "stupid and trite" by Hurston and critics. She knew she could do better: by October 1931, she had a script, Bahamian dancers, and black singers for what she called a "concert in the raw." Unlike in most shows, Hurston made a point to cast performers who were dark skinned, celebrating their "dusky, down-home glory." The revue was called *The Great Day*, and featured "dancers [who had] not been influenced by Harlem or Broadway" in order to present "true Negro music, not highly concertized spirituals."

With Godmother's unexpected blessing, the first performance occurred on January 10, 1932, at the John Golden Theatre. The show was a tremendous artistic sensation. The *Herald Tribune* wrote: "The evening was altogether successful ... and carried off with a verve, a lack of self-consciousness, and obvious spontaneous enjoyment, as eloquent as it was refreshing." However, despite positive reviews, the play was a financial flop, and Godmother had to begrudgingly absolve Hurston's debts.

Hurston would produce plays during the 1930s to great critical success, but little monetary success. This photograph of an opening night at the Lafayette Theatre, Harlem, depicts the public's fervor for theater.

Hurston tried again that same year with *From Sun to Sun*, on March 29 at the New School in New York. The playbill included scenes from *The Great Day* and a new one-act play, *The Fiery Chariot*. The performance was a brilliant success yet also failed to turn a profit. This was the last straw for Godmother. Hurston, sensing her time was up, requested a few final provisions: settlement of outstanding bills, a new pair of shoes, and money to return home to Eatonville.

RETURN TO FICTION

While Godmother had not explicitly shut the door, Hurston was determined to ween herself off her assistance, and thus, her restrictions. Hurston continued to pursue theater, arranging performances and dances across southern Florida. Boyd writes that while her "folk concerts were personally fulfilling and critically successful, they were rather sporadic and nearly as unprofitable in Florida as they'd been in New York." So Hurston returned to writing fiction, something she had not done since 1926.

She first wrote "The Gilded Six-Bits," one of her best stories. An "ironic account of infidelity and its human effects," the story instantly struck a chord with Bob Wunsch, the drama director at Rollins College. The two had previously collaborated on concerts, but he was so impressed by Hurston's literary piece that he sent it to colleagues at *Story* magazine. While they could only pay $20 for including the story in the August 1933 issue, the publicity caught the eye of Bertram Lippincott, editor at J. B. Lippincott & Co. publishing. He sent Hurston a letter asking if she was working on a novel, to which she responded in the affirmative although "not the first word was on paper."

Writing Books

Hurston had wanted to write a novel previously but said, "The idea of attempting a book seemed so big, that I gazed at it in the quiet of the night, [and] hid it away from even myself in the daylight." She began writing on July 1 and finished *Jonah's Gourd Vine* on September 6. Then, Hurston borrowed $20 from the local Daughters of the Elks club for postage to send the draft to Lippincott. By October 16, she received an acceptance letter and a $200 advance.

Hurston was alight with passion. She began hammering out *Mules and Men*, the long-awaited summation of her anthropological findings. Taking a less scientific and more reader-friendly approach, the manuscript closely followed Hurston's experiences in Eatonville, Polk Country, and New Orleans. By the time *Jonah's Gourd Vine* was published in May of 1934, Lippincott had already accepted *Mules and Men*.

Hurston quit her side jobs to focus on writing, including a short-lived position as drama department chair at the Bethune-Cookman College. It was all for the best—*Mules and Men* needed an additional sixty-five thousand words to fit within the book format. During this time, she submitted to the anthology *Negro*, applied (albeit, unsuccessfully) for a Guggenheim grant, published fiction in *Challenge* magazine, and even went to Chicago to see a performance of her folk concert, *Singing Steel*. In mid-December, she was awarded the Rosenwald Fellowship for doctoral studies at Columbia University, and as she prepared to move, Hurston remarked, "Life has picked me up bodacious and throwed me over the fence."

However, when Hurston arrived in New York, the Rosenwald Foundation revoked her scholarship. A representative told Franz Boas that Hurston's "over-zealousness" and "lack of tendency to serious quiet scholarship" distressed the foundation. They cut her funding from $3,000 to $700. Hurston, who had already enrolled for the spring semester, took the money and stopped attending classes. She was a renowned anthropologist, celebrated dramatist, essayist, and novelist: she no longer needed to be "quiet" to get where she wanted to be.

Then, for the first time in her life, Hurston fell in love. Or, as she described, "I did not just fall in love. I made a parachute jump." The man of her affection was twenty-three-year-old Percy Punter, a performer in *The Great Day*. Hurston, forty-four years old at the time, was charmed by his good looks and sharp mind, noting, "When a man keeps beating me to the draw mentally, he begins to get glamorous." Hurston was a sight to behold as well: she exuded confidence, sex appeal, and, as Boyd describes, a "funky elegance." While the two were platonic in 1932, they reconnected in 1935 and started a passionate romance, one Hurston would call "the real love affair of my life." They discussed everything, from religion, to art, to literature. Hurston began to make room for him in her life, cooking for him at home and inviting him to events on the town. However, Punter soon became jealous of Hurston's commitment to her work. He asked her to do the impossible: give it all up for him. While Hurston was fine with marriage and leaving New York, giving up her career was "that one thing [that she] could not do."

They continued to see each other, but jealousy took its toll. They fought over the smallest infractions, and Hurston recalled, "We were alternately the happiest people in the world and the most miserable." Then, one night, Hurston slapped Punter, and Punter slapped back. This was the end for the two lovers. Hurston remarked, "Our bitterest enemies could have not contrived more exquisite a torture for us."

SYNTHESIS

In October 1935, Hurston became a drama coach for the **Works Progress Administration (WPA)**, the federal program that employed Americans to work on public projects during the Great Depression. The same month, *Mules and Men* was published to

Children living in modern day Canaan, Haiti.

critical acclaim. Her two successful books proved that anthropology did not need to be presented in a drab way to be powerful. This confirmed that Hurston's true passion was writing. Boyd describes:

> From now on, she would employ her secondary career interest, anthropology, to serve what she had decided was her primary purpose: telling stories that reflected the truth, as she knew it, of black people lives.

Jamaica and Haiti

Hurston had applied for a Guggenheim grant without success in 1933, but tried again now that she was an accomplished author. On

March 30, 1936, the foundation awarded her $2,000 to conduct a "study of magic practices among Negroes in the West Indies."

Just two weeks later, Hurston arrived in Jamaica. She found the culture, still under British rule, to be unnerving. To her, everyone was in a "frantic stampede white-ward," trying to deny their "negro" qualities while looking down on darker-skinned individuals. The natives' attitudes toward women were also disturbing: most men felt a woman's only purpose was to please a man because they lacked the mental or spiritual capacity to do anything else. Despite these appalling sentiments, Hurston learned "weird and wonderful things" from escaped slaves in the mountains, hunted wild boars, and gathered more conjuring materials.

On September 22, Hurston sailed to Haiti, where she discovered the incredibly complex practice of voodoo. The material was so rich and overwhelming that Hurston applied for another Guggenheim grant. Meanwhile, she started another novel, using her reflections on her love affair with Punter as fodder. This would become her most famous novel: *Their Eyes Were Watching God*. Hurston sent the manuscript to Lippincott in December 1936 and returned to New York in March 1937. There she received great news: her book would be published in the fall and her Guggenheim grant had been extended.

On May 23, Hurston returned to the lush and mystic land of Haiti. She found so much material that she likened condensing it all to "explaining the planetary theory on a postage stamp." She felt the Haitian people were "drenched in kindliness and beaming out with charm." However, the deeper she reasearched the dark side of voodoo, the more she placed herself in danger. Hurston was close to discovering how to make zombies when she fell desperately ill. For two weeks, she was unable to leave her bed, certain she was dying from the effects of poison or the supernatural. However, she persevered and by mid-August resumed researching less dangerous subjects. She returned to New York in late September, just weeks after *Their Eyes Were Watching*

Hurston plays a traditional drum during her fieldwork in the Caribbean.

God hit the shelves. When she arrived, the book was already a phenomenal success.

Whirlwind

From 1938 to 1941, Hurston's life was a whirlwind of publications and high profile appearances. She made her home everywhere: from New York, to Jamaica, to Florida. As usual, she wrote, produced concerts, and researched. She even married again, to the twenty-three-year old Albert Prince III, but left him after six weeks and divorced him soon after. She worked for the Federal Writers' Project (FWP), scouting out folklore locations in the south for an audio-collecting team. She wrote for a host of publications: the *Saturday Review*, the *Florida Negro*, the *Saturday Evening Post*, the *American Mercury*, and more. She even served as faculty at the North Carolina College for Negroes from 1939 to early 1940.

Most impressively, Hurston published two more critically acclaimed books. *Tell My Horse*, published in 1938, was a narrative account of her conjuring and voodoo experiences in Jamaica and Haiti. Her most experimental book, *Moses, Man of the Mountain*, used the Old Testament story as an allegory to explore race in America and the philosophical idea of freedom.

In 1941, Hurston moved to California to concentrate on her autobiography, *Dust Tracks on a Road*. On October 29, she was hired by Paramount Studios, for an impressive $100 a week, as a "writer and technical advisor." While this was her largest paycheck yet, Hurston was not seduced by Hollywood. She remained in Los Angeles for Christmas, spending time with friend and performer Ethel Waters, and then resigned from Paramount on New Years Day. She then trekked across the country, stopping to lecture, until she made it back to Florida.

Living on the Water

For the first time ever, Lippincott sent Hurston serious revisions on her autobiography. She removed inflammatory statements about race and America, as well as a chapter about friendship. She regretted these omissions, especially the latter because it made her seem ungrateful, like "a hog under an acorn tree guzzling without ever looking up to see where the acorns came from." Despite these issues, Hurston published *Dust Tracks on a Road* to great popularity. She became an overnight celebrity and was bestowed the John Ansifield Award in Racial Relations and a $1,000 prize from the *Saturday Review of Literature*.

With this money, Hurston fulfilled a lifelong dream of owning a home. Like Hurston, even her home was unconventional: the *Wanago*, as in "want to go," was a 32-foot-long (10-meter-long), 44-horsepower houseboat. Hurston enjoyed the freedom and solitude of life on the water. There, she wrote the essay "High John De Conquerer" for the *American Mercury*, a mixture of thoughts on race and World War II–inspired patriotism. Hurston also participated in "Recreation in War," a program designed to entertain troops in Florida. Her third and final marriage was to Cleveland businessman James Howell Pitts. The two married in January 1944 and divorced by October. If Hurston felt any heartbreak, she didn't let on: while on the houseboat, she declared she was "the happiest [she] have ever been before in [her] life."

DIFFICULTIES AHEAD

Hurston continued to write new manuscripts, but Lippincott rejected them all. She became a contributing editor to *Negro Digest* but, hungry for more work, decided to move back to Harlem. While in New York, she supported the congressional campaign of black republican Grant Reynolds. She organized a program called "Block Mothers," where one mother would take care of all the block's children for a day as a way to help single and working mothers. "It's the old idea," she told the Barnard alumni magazine, "of helping people help themselves that will be the only salvation of the Negro in this country." Hurston became interested in politics and urged women not to become apathetic or, whether black or white, "vote as their husbands do without questioning the issues involved." She wrote articles for the *New York Tribune*, *New York World-Telegram*, and *Holiday* magazine. Just as she felt her luck and cash were running out, she met Max Perkins, editor at Charles Scribner and Sons. After two meetings, Hurston walked away with a book deal, a $5,000 advance, and a new publisher.

Honduras

On May 4, 1947, Hurston set sail for Honduras. Happy to be somewhere peaceful, she set to work on her new novel. On June 20, she sent draft pages to her literary agent who informed her that Max Perkins, at age sixty-two, had died. Hurston was deeply saddened by the news, especially since she had felt "tremendous exaltation" to be working with the renowned editor. However, her next editor, Burroughs Mitchell, was kind and astute, sending her praise and insightful edits. Hurston eventually found time to conduct research in Honduras, but she returned to the United States on February 20, 1948, to work with the editor. The new novel was titled *Seraph on the Suwanee* and was slated for an October release. She spent a few weeks in New York and then headed to the Hudson River town of Rhinebeck for the summer. On September 9, Burroughs wrote to her, requesting she come early to Manhattan to discuss publicity and future works.

Accusations

Then, the unthinkable happened: On September 13, 1948, Hurston was arrested under suspicion of molesting three schoolboys. She was taken into policy custody and questioned by detectives and a representative of the New York Society for the Prevention of Cruelty to Children. The allegations were completely false: she was accused of committing crimes in New York while she was in Honduras (she even had the passport to prove it.) Hurston's editor and attorney bailed her out, assuring her the case was too crazy to move forward. They decided to release her new book, *Seraph on the Suwanee*, as scheduled.

Unfortunately, the charade carried on. Hurston had told the police when she had returned to Harlem, and suddenly the alleged dates changed from the previous year to the previous month. Hurston said that was when "the horror took me, for I saw that he was not seeking the truth, but to make his charges stick … I could not believe that a thing like this could be happing in the United States and least of all to me." While *Seraph on the Suwanee* received good reviews, it didn't take long for the tabloids to publish crude headlines. Hurston was distraught: she halted all book dealings, moved to the Bronx, and fell into a deep depression. She lived in isolation until March 1949, when the trial was finally dismissed: the boys had admitted to lying. While most people didn't believe the slanderous and ridiculous accusations, the trauma had taken its toll. Hurston went to the brink of despair and even contemplated suicide, but when it was all over, she had a clean slate and a broken heart.

After the trial, Hurston moved back to Miami to recover. By January 1950, she had written a new novel, published more articles, and started speaking in public again. However, she was in debt from legal fees and had to work as a maid for a wealthy white couple. Her employer recognized her, told her friends, and eventually recounted the story to the local papers. Hurston shrewdly used the publicity to her advantage, saying she needed to "shift gears" and that "[a] writer has to stop writing every now and then and

The original manuscript of *Seraph on the Suwanee* at the University of Florida's library. This and many other papers were saved from being burned after Hurston's death.

just live a little." This generated a boost in sales and work for the next few months, allowing Zora to quit the maid business for good.

Scribner's eventually canned her novel in progress, *Barney Turk*. Hurston stayed optimistic and continued to work: she wrote an anti-communism essay for the *American Legion* and moved to Eau Gallie, Florida, to focus on a new, "truly negro novel," tentatively called *The Golden Bench of God*. Scribner's rejected this as well, despite how well *Seraph on the Suwanee* was still selling. Hurston then started writing a small column for the *Weekly Review* in August, Georgia.

Her last big break, however, was from the *Pittsburg Courier*, a nationally distributed periodical. Hurston would cover the most notorious trial of 1952: Ruby McCollum, a black woman, had shot and killed a white, married doctor with whom she was having an affair. This ten-part series was some of Hurston's best writing from the 1950s. She eventually brought in William Bradford Huie, a white reporter, to give a more balanced perspective. In the end, McCollum was spared a death sentence, most likely thanks to Hurston's work.

From King Herod to Death

In 1953, Hurston started writing a book on King Herod. To support herself, she helped Huie write his book about Ruby McCollum, ghost wrote a book, and lectured. On June 3, 1955, she sent in her Herod manuscript, only to be rejected again. However, Hurston was completely unfazed. She wrote controversial op-eds for the *Orlando Sentinel* and other papers. She also worked as a librarian at the Patrick Air Force Base but was fired for being "too well educated," a relief since Hurston felt the job was boring. In 1948, she began teaching in a high school in Fort Pierce, all the while revising her King Herod manuscript.

Then, Hurston finally had to stop writing: in May 1959, she suffered a stroke, and in October, she was transferred to a nursing home. Her doctor recalled that "she really couldn't write much near the end … [The stroke] left her weak; her mind was affected. She couldn't think about anything for long." Yet Hurston, as always, remained an optimist. Her brother Joel, his wife, and their daughter Vivian often visited, and Hurston always told them she was happy and contented. When they asked her if she was afraid of dying, she responded, "Why fear? The stuff of my being is matter, ever changing, ever moving, but never lost."

On Thursday, January 28, 1960, Hurston had another stroke. She was pronounced dead upon arrival at the hospital, just as the sun had set in the sky.

PART II

The Work of Zora Neale Hurston

"Those that don't got it, can't show it. Those that got it, can't hide it."

—*Zora Neale Hurston*

Opposite: A collection of Hurston's letters was published posthumously, further illuminating the difference between the author's public and private personas.

CHAPTER FOUR

DIVERSITY

In her extremely prolific and versatile career, Zora Neale Hurston would write many different types of pieces: short stories, anthropological findings, personal essays, scripts, novels, journalistic articles, and editorials. This is a dizzying array of genres, each with a different form and purpose, and might have seemed scattered if not for Hurston's focused approach. By using specific techniques and subject matter, as well as a strong narrative voice, Hurston provided a solid through-line in her diverse body of work.

Techniques

Hurston's novels, in particular, often take the form of a **roman à clef**. French for "novel with a key," this refers to a novel that is based on real life but overlaid with fictional elements. The "key" is the relationship between reality and fiction: a layer of meaning lies between what has been changed from real life and why. Often this technique is employed for political satire, anonymity, or to avoid legal complications in

Opposite: Zora Neale Hurston and an unknown man in Belle Glade, Florida.

regard to the subject matter. Hurston, however, utilized this technique for an entirely different purpose: authenticity.

To bring to light the undocumented or misunderstood folkways of various black cultures, Hurston plucked most of her dialogue straight from the mouths of real people. All of her stories made use of **eye dialect**, or the purposeful misspelling of words to imply the sound, pronunciation, and cadence of a character's speech. For example, in her first short story, "John Redding Goes to Sea," the main character's father, Alfred, defends his son with sentences constructed entirely of eye dialect: "Matty, let dat boy alone, Ah tell you! Ef he wuz uh home-buddy he'd be drove 'way by you all's racket."

By emphasizing these speech patterns in characters' dialogue, Hurston could represent the unique sounds and personality of native Floridians. These turns of phrase change when documenting other **diasporic communities**, or communities descended from the historic movement of African people during the slave trade. In *Tell My Horse,* Hurston recorded a Haitian describing a zombie: "We have examples of a man who gave salt to a demon by mistake and he come man again and can write the name of the man who gave him to the [voodoo spirit]." Though subtle, Hurston tried to capture the delineations and inventions inherent in different characters' speech. The result was richly layered texts that were imbued with the colors and flavors of a seemingly native, authentic culture.

In addition to language, Hurston utilized the roman á clef technique in the more traditional sense: pulling from larger narratives and experiences in her own life. Her anthropological novels have been coined as "auto-ethnographic," meaning they blended autobiography with **ethnography**, the scientific description of customs of a culture of people.

Even in fictional works, like *Their Eyes Were Watching God,* Hurston uses characters, settings, and events from her own life. The founder of fictional Eatonville is Jody Starks, a thinly veiled version of Eatonville's real mayor, Joe Clarke. The main character, Janie Mae Crawford, has two unsuccessful marriages before falling in love with Tea Cake, a young man twelve years her junior. When Hurston wrote this novel, she herself had already had one unsuccessful marriage and had fallen deeply in love with the young Percy Punter. The characters also experience a devastating hurricane, something Hurston also witnessed while in the Bahamas. The list of similarities goes on, further emphasizing Hurston's desire to make literature out of her own experiences.

While the authenticity of her experiences rings true, it is her storytelling that elevates them to the realm of art. In her fiction, Hurston organizes a lifetime of experiences into defined narratives with dramatic arcs. Characters grow, plots are driven by actions, and there is a larger sense of meaning due to her use of an eloquent third person narrator. She peppers these diverse life experiences with literary references, philosophy, and naturalistic imagery, all while revealing that her subject matter, ordinary black lives, is just as poignant and beautiful as the classic topics of high-class literature.

SHORT STORIES

The short story format first provided Hurston a realm to explore her ideas of "art as life." Throughout her career she often returned to this form to regain her creative footing and crystallize her ideas. It was also one of her more profitable formats: stories were concise pieces that were able to be published in different magazines and publications, and sometimes even reprinted for a small fee. Most of her life Hurston was one of the few black, female authors in America making a living from her writing, partly thanks to her short stories.

Hurston's first short story was "John Redding Goes to Sea," published in Howard University's literary club magazine *Stylus* in May 1921. Set in an unnamed Florida village, modeled after her own Eatonville, the story follows a "queer child," who dreams of taking a steam boat down the St. John's River and traveling the world. John's father sympathizes with him while his mother scorns his foolishness. We follow John through a life that beats him down: each time he attempts to leave, his family guilts him into staying, first his mother and then his wife. He takes a job building a bridge that will cross the St. John's, until a thunderstorm strikes him while working. In the end, John is set free by death, floating away on debris:

> His arms were outstretched, and the water washed over his [shoes] but his feet were lifted out of the water whenever the timber was buoyed up by the stream … Out on the bosom of the river, bobbing up and down as if waving good bye, piloting his little craft on the shining river road, John Redding floated away toward Jacksonville, the sea, the wide world—at last.

Readers responded to the story's combination of low and high elements: while characters appear raw and use crude language, they also play into a larger allegory. Hurston also utilized common superstitions in the black community. On the night of John Redding's death, an owl is heard screeching, something his mother remarks is a "sho' sign uh death." In the end, the tragedy of John Redding's life is almost biblical: his death scene is likened to being crucified on the cross.

History has since regarded this story as one of Hurston's more juvenile works. The characterization has been described as heavy handed and the allegorical allusions overwrought. However, as a first attempt, it makes clear Hurston's intention as an author: bring the ordinary black experience into the dialogue of literature.

"Sweat"

Published in *Fire!!* in November 1926, "Sweat" is one of Hurston's most striking stories. Delia Jones, a washerwoman in a rural Florida town, works diligently to sort clothes on a Sunday evening. She is soon disturbed by her "strapping hulk" of a husband, Sykes, who throws his bullwhip at her to frighten her into thinking it's a snake. She chides him for the trickery, and in retaliation he begins to dirty the clothes, kicking them and mixing the darks with the light. For once, Delia gathers the strength to banish him from the house. He leaves, but Delia knows where he's headed: right into the arms of Bertha, a curvaceous woman who is the visual opposite of Delia. This allows Delia to reflect on her sad fifteen years of marriage, taking physical and mental abuse from her husband while working to support them both. Sykes continues to run around town with Bertha, prominently showing her off to the townsfolk who gossip about his repulsive behavior.

Then, the final straw: Sykes catches a real-life rattlesnake and brings it home, just to scare Delia. In a flurry of broken words, Delia tells her husband, "Ah hates you tuh de same degree dat Ah useter love yuh." The couple no longer pretends to be cordial, Delia avoiding anywhere she might run into him, and Sykes showing off both his snake and new woman. One night, Delia starts to sort clothes on the bed instead of the floor, a luxury she never afforded herself while subject to Sykes's wrath. Suddenly, the 6-foot (2 m) rattlesnake appears under the laundry. Delia sprints from the house to the barn and waits for hours, eventually falling asleep on the hay.

When she awakes she creeps to the house, seeing from the outside that Sykes has returned. He searches for a match to light the lamp when he hears the snake's rattling. Sykes, in his fear, leaps

A woman washing laundry in Putnam County, Georgia. Hurston used this colloquial archetype in her story "Sweat." She would later visit and study locals in Putnam.

to the bed. Then, Delia hears horrible sounds coming from the room. After a long while, Delia comes to the door to see Sykes, swollen and dying, calling out her name. She calmly retreats to the chinaberry tree in the backyard and waits for the sun to rise on her new life, while the sun sets on Sykes.

The story is overtly feminist: a woman who has been emotionally and physically repressed by her husband is finally released once she declares her independence. Delia's profession, that of a washerwoman, is symbolic: she desires order and to rid her life of its dirt and grime. Furthermore, washing clothes was a physically back-breaking career that paid very little—another form of oppression, as well as a testament to the ordinary woman's strength and perseverance. Using the biblical imagery of the snake as a symbol of sin and evil, Sykes is eventually destroyed by his own malicious deeds and pride. The final image, that of the chinaberry tree, deserves a nuanced reading as well. While it provides shade and a peaceful spot to linger, its fruit is actually poisonous. Through its use of symbols, natural language, and a concise plot, "Sweat" is a haunting tale about love, hate, and independence.

ANTHROPOLOGY

Hurston's work grew in spades when at Barnard she started studying with professor Franz Boas, the man considered to be the father of modern anthropology. Historically, anthropologists studied civilizations by directly comparing them to Western, Eurocentric societies. The further a culture was away from this "standard," the more it was judged as "uncivilized," or wrong. This is known as **ethnocentricity**, or the belief that one's own culture is inherently superior to another by nature. This prevailing thought made for anthropology that at times was little more than racist **diatribes**.

Boas, however, had a different approach: **cultural relativism**. Though the term was coined later, the principle states that to understand a culture, one must view it through that culture's own lens. He argued that "civilization is not something absolute, but that it is relative, and that our ideas and conceptions are true only so far as our civilization goes." As a scientist, an anthropologist's prerogative was to try to see things from another culture's perspective. The best way to do so, Boas believed, was by conducting fieldwork or research alongside native peoples. Hurston adhered strongly to Boas's teachings on how to research but, unlike most anthropologists, found her own approach to presenting her findings.

Mules and Men

The 247-page book, published in 1935, is divided into two sections: the first, a nonfiction account of Hurston's travels through Eatonville and Polk County, and the second, her experience with hoodoo in New Orleans. Unusual in its blending of travel anecdotes, folk stories, songs, and even recipes, Mules and Men provided a reader-friendly entry into Southern culture. It is a book that can be read as a narrative or as a bibliography for **primary sources**, meaning the original artifacts for a source of information being studied.

Though much of the book is spent documenting and reproducing stories, Hurston does draw her own ethnographic conclusions. Scholar Babacar M'Baye writes that Hurston realized the "concealed and resistive nature of folklore in the **African Diaspora**" is what allowed it to sustain, and evolve, over the years. Many themes and fables appear to be direct descendents of African lore: in the South, many of the fables she collected about Brer Rabbit bear strong resemblance to Senegalese and West African myths. Yet, what she discovered was not just strictly African influences: many of the popular "figure dances" of Polk County were influenced by French and English dances. Furthermore, many of the stories and games carried themes relevant to the black American experience: the importance of traditions, respect, spirituality, and resistance to oppression. Most excitingly, Hurston noted that "Negro folk-lore is still in the making. A new kind is crowding out the old one."

Learning Hoodoo

Before Hurston's research, there were no comprehensive studies on hoodoo in America. What did exist often belittled it: in the 1926 book *Folk Beliefs of the Southern Negro*, white southerner Newbell Niles Puckett mockingly described conjuring as "a rather unsophisticated con game that could be exposed by any rational person." Puckett disguised himself as a conjure doctor, handing out fake cures and communicating with other doctors who most likely fed him false information because of his obvious charade. Many white Louisianans in the 1920s believed in hoodoo's effectiveness, although mainly black and Creole populations practiced it. Puckett's race, performance, and general ignorance of hoodoo would have been red flags to any true believer.

Hurston's approach would be completely different. She came to hoodoo without preconceived notions or assumptions and desired to know more about the practice. To learn the rites and rituals of hoodoo, she would need to apprentice herself to a master, but before she could do that, she needed to find the most knowledgeable hoodoo doctors of all New Orleans. Most hoodoo doctors in New Orleans claimed to have a connection to Marie Laveau, the renowned Creole conjurer. Said to have walked on water and commanded a giant snake, Marie Laveau was a mysterious, but respected, magician. Anyone who wanted to legitimize his or her hoodoo abilities in the Crescent City seemed to be related to her or to have trained under her. Hurston met a diverse range of these doctors: male and female, old and young. Each one required payment, both monetarily and spiritually through submission to rigorous initiation rites. If Hurston could successfully accomplish these tests, she would prove herself worthy.

She witnessed and participated in a host of strange and exotic rituals. The "Black Cat Bone" ritual required Hurston to catch a cat, throw it in boiling water, and pass several of its bones through her mouth until she had found a bitter one. Then, in a rather vague description, Hurston wrote some "unearthly terror" took hold as "indescribable noises, sights, [and] feelings" passed through her. "Before the day," she concluded, "I was home with a small white bone for me to carry." She then studied under Father Watson, known as the "Frizzly Rooster," for his ability to remove curses, his nickname referring to his ability to use country chickens to unearth any buried backyard hexes. Once becoming his pupil, Hurston was initiated as a "Boss of Candles," meaning she could "work with spirits anywhere on earth" without the help of another doctor. Hurston performed intricate rituals with Watson, including tying the hands of a doll behind its back to, as Boyd describes, lessen "a popular preacher's blind ambition."

It wasn't until she came under the tutelage of Luke Turner, who claimed to be Laveau's nephew, that Hurston would be truly tested. Turner, after a tense spiritual examination, was so convinced of Hurston's worthiness that he refused to accept payment. Instead, he taught her how to "crown the spirit of death." For nine nights, she slept with her right stocking on and her left leg bare. She wrote, "I must have clean thoughts. I must neither defile body nor spirit." After this, she undressed and lay face down on Turner's couch, which had been covered in rattlesnake skins, for three days and three nights. Hurston was unable to eat, but was allowed water so that, Boyd writes, "her soul would not wander off in search of water and risk being attacked by evil influences." This religious **asceticism**, or the act of severe self-discipline and avoiding indulgences, was intended to bring her to a greater level of spiritual understanding. After sixty-nine hours and five psychic experiences, Hurston awoke from her experience with "no feelings of hunger, only one of exaltation."

Hurston had stepped across the threshold from researcher, to believer, to practitioner. She once wrote, "Belief in magic is older than writing," asserting that humans need spiritualism as much as

ZOMBIES

Western culture has been fascinated with the zombie since the early twentieth century. However, long before it was a pop culture icon, the zombie was a very real and terrifying thing for voodoo practitioners. Derived from the Kongo word *nzambi,* meaing "spirit of the dead person," the Haitain zombie is a person who has been brought back to life by black magic to serve another's will. Aaron Mahnke, host of Lore Podcast, describes how colonial Haitians believed that the "soul and body were connected, but also that death could be a moment of separation between the two." Furthermore, Haitians lived in "hatred and fear of slavery." If a person wanted to employ dark magic to make another suffer, than the greatest punishment would be "eternal imprisonment inside their own body, without control or power over themselves … a slavery that went on forever." Hurston had the rare opportunity to see and touch one of these trapped souls known as a zombie:

> I listened to the broken noises in its throat … The sight was dreadful. That blank face with the dead eyes. The eyelids were white all around the eyes as if they had been burned with acid … There was nothing you could say to her, or get from her, except by looking at her, and the sight of this wreckage was too much to endure for long.

Hurston wrote that, had she not experienced this in daylight, she would have been doubtful. However, she had seen with her own eyes a woman who had been "called back from the dead."

they need a language for expression. Hurston was now the only person to have experienced hoodoo so deeply and possess the academic and literary skills to write about it. However, because she respected these private and mystic ways, she did not spill all the secrets. Boyd, says, "The balancing act required a double consciousness—that of a conjurer and that of a chronicler."

THEATER

Hurston had always felt that "Negro material [was] eminently suited to drama and music." Scientific writing failed to capture the drama so essential to the folk oral tradition. More than this, science could only document the spirit of the thing, not express it. Theater, performance, and concerts became to Hurston a lively way to bring her material to life.

While Hurston wrote many brilliant skits, concerts, and plays, she never achieved financial success with her productions during her lifetime. Most attribute this to the Great Depression: in the midst of nationwide financial ruin, theater seemed like an extravagance few could support. While audiences were engaged with the material, the nature of theater requires monetary support to survive.

Mule Bone

Mule Bone: A Comedy of Negro Life is Hurston's best-known play, though unfortunately due to its controversy rather than the story itself. Based on an Eatonville story, the three-act play follows locals Dave and Jim as they fight over a woman named Daisy's affection. The two men come to blows, and Jim picks up a mule bone he finds on the ground and knocks out Dave. Jim is eventually arrested, and the second act follows the comical question of the trial: is it considered assault if an attack is made by something that is not a weapon? Does a mule bone in fact count as a weapon? Colorful language ensues, but the trial concludes with evidence against

Jim: a Bible passage that says Samson used a donkey's bone to kill three thousand men. Jim is convicted as guilty and banished from town. The third act details a chance meeting of Daisy and Jim, followed by another coincidence as Dave stumbles upon the couple. The two men take turns arguing over who is more worthy of Daisy then the other. As Daisy chimes in, she makes it clear she expects the winner to work for the same white employers she does. With that, it is over: neither man is interested, and the two return to Eatonville, thick as thieves once more.

NOVELS

Surprisingly, Godmother gave one bit of good advice before she dismissed Hurston: "In all that you do, Zora, remember it is vital to your people that you should not rob your books, which must stand as a lasting monument, in order to further a commercial venture." In this way, she was right: it was through novels that Hurston would see her greatest successes.

Their Eyes Were Watching God

Hurston's most famous novel, *Their Eyes Were Watching God*, published in 1937, is an American classic. Janie Crawford, an attractive, confident, middle-aged woman, has made a stir in the town of Eatonville. After years of absence, she has returned alone, without her young husband, Tea Cake. The town gossips about Janie's young clothes and missing husband, but her friend Pheoby Watson defends her and heads to her home to hear what happens. Janie begins the conversation that frames the novel.

When Janie was young, her mother ran off, so she was raised by her grandmother. Her "nanny" was loving and dedicated, but her life as a slave had made her afraid for Janie. Knowing she wouldn't always be around to help her, she married Janie off to a much older, but secure, farmer named Logan Killicks. Hurston's narrative voice frame's Janie's worry: "There are years that ask questions and years that answer. Janie had had no chance to know things, so she had to ask. Did marriage end the cosmic loneliness of the unmated? Did marriage compel love like the sun the day?"

Unfortunately, after moving in with Logan, she realizes it does not: he is unromantic, practical, and treats her like an employee on the farm. One day, she runs off with another man named Joe "Jody" Starks, with whom she will spend twenty years in a loveless marriage. He becomes mayor of an all-black town called Eatonville and, as he gains more power, becomes more of a controlling figure in Janie's life. One day, he insults her body, and Janie decides to leave him. Soon after, Jody falls deathly ill and passes away.

When Jody passes, Janie feels an immense sense of freedom. She denies all the various suitors who come knocking until a man named Tea Cake, twelve years her junior, walks into the shop. The sparks fly instantly—Janie has never felt such chemistry with another man, and Tea Cake reciprocates. The town gossips about the scandalous union, but the two could care less. Then, to everyone's surprise, Janie remarries Tea Cake and leaves for Jacksonville, only nine months after Jody's death.

During their first week of marriage, an incident occurs that leaves Janie thinking the rumors around town had been real: Tea Cake was only after her money and was waiting to run off the first chance he got. However, Tea Cake proves it all to be a misunderstanding and promises to be open with her from now on. They move to the Everglades and work during the harvest season, socializing in the off seasons. Their life together is full of fun, music, and love: Janie finally has all that she's ever wanted.

They have many good years, but it all comes crashing to an end when a terrible hurricane rips through the Everglades. The following scenes are full of beautiful and terrifying images of destruction and fear—huddling for dear life, the couple and their friends try to escape the winds and a tidal wave. As they flee the rising waters, a dog attacks Janie. Tea Cake saves her, but in the end is bitten. They escape, and all seems well until, three weeks

Their Eyes Were Watching God has become Zora Neale Hurston's most beloved book and is often featured on reading lists and course syllabi.

later, Tea Cake starts acting strangely. Janie calls the doctor and he tells her the terrible truth: Tea Cake has contracted rabies. He will die of it, possibly becoming violent. As soon as the doctor leaves, the diagnosis comes true: delusional, Tea Cake thinks Janie is cheating on him and starts firing at her. In a dramatic drawing of guns, Janie is forced to kill Tea Cake to save him from his madness.

Almost instantly she is put on trial. The black folks seem to glare and desire her hanging, but the all-white, all-male jury finds her not guilty. Janie returns to Eatonille to the snickers and sneers of town gossip. However, as Janie finishes her account to Pheoby, she assures her that she has never been happier. Later that night, when Janie is alone in her room, she wraps herself in a shawl and remembers her happy life, finally at peace.

This novel was one of the first times a black female protagonist was shown living her life according to her own terms, and without apology. As such, it was hugely inspirational for generations of African-American women and feminists, and often drew criticism from those who disagreed with Janie's fierce independence.

CHAPTER FIVE

COMPLEXITIES

As an author, Hurston was a jack-of-all-trades and extremely prolific. In all her work, she asserted a strong, unshakable vision about race and human character. As such, she has been both lionized and vilified. Her work was simultaneously praised and criticized, her opinions seen as both forward thinking and conservative. Hurston lived by her own design: she said what she thought and did what she wanted, regardless of anyone else's opinion. This is often casually said of many people, but with Hurston it was an undeniable truth. At times it cost her friends, and for a while, it seemed it would rob her of her historical importance. However, time has restored Hurston to her rightful place, and many scholars and writers have written about the merits and challenges of her work.

Opposite: Hurston beating a *hountar*, or mama drum. This image embodies the controversy surrounding Hurston: Did she earnestly integrate herself into her subjects' lives, or did she dramatize them for an outside audience?

FOLK MATERIAL: FACT OR FICTION

Hurston's anthropological contributions have been invaluable to understanding the lives of African Americans in the first half of the twentieth century. She received accolades within her lifetime for her efforts and was a member of the American Ethnological Society and the Anthropological Society. When she was working in the field, she was considered the foremost expert on black folk culture. The very act of bringing attention to this material was revolutionary, as scholar Sharon Lynette Jones writes: "By retelling black folk stories, which often focus on animals and common people, and by presenting the beauty and complexity of dialect of the black vernacular, or African-American English, Hurston was implicitly validating a literary tradition that had long been considered secondary."

Unconventional Methods

If Hurston's subject matter was new to the general public, then her methods of interpretation were almost unheard of. Unlike her colleagues, Hurston did not present her findings in an overly academic or formal way. In fact, it was quite the opposite: her collections, like *Mules and Men* and *Tell My Horse*, alternate between ethnographic findings and travel narratives. Though Hurston strove to be **empirical**, guided by information gained through observation or experience, she was not a completely neutral or invisible observer. Her approach to fieldwork was rooted in **reflexivity,** a concept in anthropology that has two meanings, both of which Hurston explored. The first refers to the researcher's awareness of their relationship to the subject matter. The second meaning of reflexivity refers to the subject's self-reflection on his or her own culture. Hurston used **participatory research**, or research gained from a partnership with the community being studied, to round out her narratives. If she needed to witness an important cultural event, participate in a ceremony, or engage in an activity, she openly asked the native people. Rather than wait or watch from a distance, she engaged with the population. Anthropologist Irma McClaurin notes Hurston did this "at a time when her colleagues viewed the people they studied as mere objects and not as people who could make contributions to the research process itself."

It was this unconventional insertion of herself into the narrative, and her direct interaction with the subjects at hand, which makes Hurston's work so challenging. Ronald E. Martin, author of *The Languages of Difference: American Writers and Anthropologists*, describes the double-edged sword of this approach:

> Hurston's personal, original perception and expression most crucially shape the text. There are scientific standards and there are literary and intellectual genres and traditions, but Hurston will have it her own way, and this enriches, complicates, and confuses her presentation of her subject and her claim to authority.

Sticking to the Facts

In Hurston's lifetime, this complicated approach was the source of much criticism. While *Mules and Men* was generally hailed as a success, *Tell My Horse* had mixed reviews. At the time, a reviewer for the *New Yorker* wrote that it was a "disorganized but interesting account of Miss Hurston's visit to Jamaica and Haiti." Alain Locke, her former mentor, wrote a scathing review in *Opportunity* magazine, dismissing the book as a source of "anthropological gossip." Martin attributes Hurston's diminished impact with *Tell My Horse* to her lack of native familiarity with the material:

> In *Tell My Horse* investigator/narrator Zora does not have the linguistic advantage that she had in *Mules and Men;* she is not a daughter of these parts ... She includes a good

deal of quotation, translation, and imitative locution … [and] often takes the liberty in this book of openly expressing her opinions and judgments.

It is the latter that other critics have honed on. Barbara Ladd, a literary and gender studies scholar, writes that *Tell My Horse* "is unlike anything else written by a U.S. writer. Not a discourse on the Caribbean per se, it is an examination of what it means to be both black and a citizen of the United States in the late 1930s." She goes on to describe the benefits of this perspective, as well as the author's failed intentions to create a treatise purely about Caribbean folklore.

FICTIONAL AUTOBIOGRAPHY

Hurston had always smudged the details of her life to fit into her own narrative. Infamous for her casual way of changing her age, at the time of her death, hardly anyone knew the truth. To avoid divulging these details in her autobiography, Hurston approached the subject of her birth as if it were a folktale itself. She begins her chapter "I Get Born" with an offhand comment about her approach to "facts": "This is all hear-say. Maybe some of the details of my birth as told me might be a little inaccurate, but it is pretty well established that I really did get born."

Author Ann Rayson notes that the book has an "overt mythic framework," and that the book is full of "tall tale–telling," something to be expected due to the "untamable vibrancy in her personality." Darwin T. Turner, in his foreword to *Dust Tracks on a Road*, acknowledges this as well, writing, "*Dust Tracks* may be the best fiction Zora Neale Hurston ever wrote."

Memoir, Not Autobiography

However, history has since applauded Hurston's unique approach to autobiography, especially in a time when the odds were

Richard Wright, one of Hurston's biggest critics

against her. In the 1940s, there were few black biographies, and almost none of them were about women. In this way, Hurston needed to set herself up for, as Rayson describes, a "special mention among men." The mythic portions of *Dust Track* do this in a bold way in order to paint her life as special and unique. Boyd points out that Hurston's male contempories, like Langston Hughes and Richard Wright, approached their own biographies in this way, although their exaggerations have been ignored, while Hurston was "vehemently [attacked] … for doing the very same thing." In this way, *Dust Tracks on a Road* is daringly feminist.

Boyd also makes a point that while during her day, Hurston's "fast and loose" use of the facts may have garnered criticism, today we would consider it more memoir than autobiography. He concludes that the memorist's job is not to capture the "letter of the life, but the spirit of it … The story of a self-invented woman, *Dust Tracks on a Road* offers a reliable account of a writer's *inner* life." Rayson agrees, saying that Hurston succeeds in "portraying her real self, which is all that any autobiographer can hope to do." Hurston's final note to the reader embodies it all:

> Well, that is the way things stand up to now. I can look back and see sharp shadows, high light, and smudgy inbetweens. I have been in Sorrow's kitchen and licked out all the pots. Then I have stood on the peaky mountain wrapped in rainbows, with a harp and sword in my hands.

"HOW IT FEELS TO BE COLORED ME"

The most controversial aspect of Hurston's work and personality was her attitude toward race. Hurston lived through half a century of changing politics, theories, and social movements that changed black lives in America. She always seemed to be on the fringe of popular ideas because of her inextinguishable sense of individuality.

While this served her well most of the time, occasionally her inflexible nature prevented her from seeing the progress that was inevitably taking place. It is without doubt that Hurston loved her culture and her people, but it was a complicated relationship.

Above all else, Hurston believed in **rugged individualism**. A term coined by President Herbert Hoover during the onset of the Great Depression, it refers to the idea that an individual should be able to pull him or herself up from poverty without assistance, especially from the government. This belief is important to the idea of the "American Dream," which says a person can have it all if they work hard enough. This made complete sense to Hurston, a woman who came from rural Florida, entered the elite world of New York City intellectuals, traveled the world, and became a celebrated author. However, this opinion took precedence over all others, including tough issues surrounding race.

Sidestepping the Issues

Hurston's first declaration of her individualism appeared in her 1928 essay "How It Feels to Be Colored Me." This is her manifesto on race: throughout her life, her opinions would rarely deviate from these sentiments. Starting with the first time she "felt colored," the essay chronicles the different instances in which she senses the implications of her race. Each time, she evaluates how race reflects on her own personality, as well as black culture on the whole. One of her first points is that she is not downtrodden by her race:

> But I am not tragically colored. There is no great sorrow dammed up in my soul, nor lurking behind my eyes … I do not belong to the sobbing school of Negrohood who hold that nature somehow has given them a lowdown dirty deal whose feelings are all about it … No, I do not weep at the world—I am too busy sharpening my oyster knife.

Hurston at a New York City book fair, circa 1937

This sentiment was not completely out of line with the message conveyed by other artists in the Harlem Renaissance. Many of Hurston's colleagues, like Langston Hughes and the artists involved in *Fire!!*, were eager to redesign the way the public saw African Americans. Instead of the "New Negro" that Locke had in mind, a black person who fit snuggly into the white ideal of sophistication, they wanted blacks to be proud of who they were. In this way, Hurston's desire not to be pitied by virtue of her race was understandable and even applauded.

However, it was Hurston's insistence that her life, and the lives of her people, could be completely unaffected by past and present racial issues that was cause for disagreement. In "How It Feels to Be Colored Me," Hurston acknowledges slavery's former chokehold on her black idenity but actually cites it as a launching point toward a greater future:

> Someone is always at my elbow reminding me that I am the granddaughter of slaves … Slavery is the price I paid for civilization and the choice was not with me. It is a bully adventure and worth all that I have paid through my ancestors for it. No one on earth ever had a greater chance for glory … It is thrilling to think—to know that for any act of mine, I shall get twice as much praise or twice as much blame.

Furthermore, Hurston insists that her white neighbors are in a far more difficult position, living with the ghosts of their shame and having to defend a world order that is destined to change. She writes, "The game of keeping what one has is never so exciting as the game of getting."

This perspective did not sit well with other black intellectuals who could easily trace the lines of slavery and its lasting effects on a segregated America. However, Hurston was not ignorant to racism and considered it white people's way of "limiting the competition" by "[rigging] the game so that they cannot lose." More importantly, Hurston had a particular way of dealing with racism: "I have met it in the flesh [but] I do not give it heart room because it seems to me to be the last refuge of the weak."

Unfavorable Politics

Hurston is often regarded as a political conservative, something that deeply aggravated her colleagues during her lifetime. While many black artists felt racial politics were central to their work, Hurston often turned away, or ignored, these issues. When *Their Eyes Were Watching God* hit the shelves, author and activist Richard Wright ripped it to shreds. He believed the novel carried "no theme, no message, no thought," partly because of its lack of political messages. Critics have since rebuked Wright's assessment, noting how his strangely regressive views on women influenced his opinion on a book that focused primarily on the internal life of a black woman. At the time, however, he spoke for many other enraged black liberals who felt Hurston's emphasis on the lighthearted and folk perpetuated an "image for the benefit of white readers." In his review of *Their Eyes Were Watching God*, Wright wrote: "[Hurston's] characters eat and laugh and cry and work and kill; they swing like a pendulum eternally in that safe and narrow orbit in which America likes to see the Negro live: between laughter and tears."

Jim Crow

This would not be the last time Hurston ignited contempt from the black community. In 1943, she was interviewed for the *New York World-Telegram*, where she openly agreed with **Jim Crow laws**, or local and state laws that enforced segregation:

Jim Crow laws allowed for legal segregation of black and white people in public places.

The lot of the Negro is much better in the South than in the North ... There is of course, segregation, no social intermingling. I can't go into certain white nightclubs or dine in first-class white hotels. But for everything put up in the South for white people there is an equivalent for the Negro. In other words, the Jim Crow system works.

For Hurston, who had grown up in all-black Eatonville, this made sense. Black folks cared for their own: there was no chance of getting the short end of the stick if the system was designed for you, by you. She had seen the effects of an imposing white presence on her Harlem colleagues, who felt disenfranchised by a culture that ignored them or thought them lesser than whites. To Hurston, the option to opt out of the whole mess made sense.

However, the world would not be moving toward more racial segregation, but toward racial inclusion. On behalf of the NAACP, Roy Wilkins wrote in response to Hurston's interview that:

Miss Hurston is a bright person with a flair for actions and sayings that yield rich publicity dividends. She gets talked about. She gets cussed and praised. All that helps the Hurston book sales ... Now is not the time for Negro writers like Zora Hurston to come out with publicity wisecracks about the South being better for the Negro than the North ... The race is fighting a battle that may determine its status for fifty years. Those who are not for us, are against us.

Brown vs. Board of Education of Topeka, Kansas

Hurston's last affront to the liberal black community was her rejection of the 1954 **Brown v. Board of Education of Topeka, Kansas** ruling, the landmark Supreme Court case that ruled segregation illegal. On August 11, 1955, Hurston wrote an

COMMUNISM

Hurston also opposed communism, an idea that was taking hold in many of the liberal Harlem circles. The idea makes sense: theoretical communism seeks to equalize everyone in social and economic standing. For a people long relegated to the bottom rungs of society, communism offered a stable and respectable position. However, Hurston was a steadfast patriot and, thus, an anti-communist. In "How It Feels to Be Colored Me," she wrote: "I have no separate feeling about being an American citizen and colored. I am merely a fragment of the Great Soul that surges within the boundaries. My country, right or wrong."

Ann Rayson goes one step further, likening Hurston to a "black female Ben Franklin" for her sense of "American individualism and moderation." While believing in communist ideals, Hurston would never be a convert: "Anyone would be a fool or a liar to claim that there was no good in it. But I am so put together that I do not have much of a herd instinct. Or if I must be connected with the flock, let *me* be the shepherd of my own self."

opinion editorial to the *Orlando Sentinel*, saying she was not against desegregation but that she objected to "forcible association." She viewed that this ruling hinted that black-run organizations needed a white presence, or that blacks needed to go to white organizations to be cared for. She wrote that the ruling was "insulting rather than honoring [to] my race," and as a result, received a lot of criticism from black activists.

Hurston's Solution

However, Hurston was not one to just denounce something without offering a solution. In her 1950 essay entitled "What White Publishers Won't Print," she also argued that racism would not end until the American culture at large took an interest in the private lives of minorities. (This article addressed different minorities—a rarity as she often only spoke to the black experience.) It would not come by reading fiction "built around upper-class Negroes exploiting the race problem," nor from stereotypical stand-ins for an entire race. Hurston stressed that the end of racism would only come from understanding the inner lives of ordinary African Americans: "The realistic story around a Negro insurance official, dentist, general practitioner, undertaker, and the like would be more revealing ... For various reasons, the average, struggling, non-morbid Negro is the best-kept secret in America."

By expressing this image, Hurston felt the culture at large could see how similar we all are to one another, thereby replacing the unkown and the feared with the relatable and loved. This sentiment is the maturation of an earlier comment Hurston made when describing her first novel, *Jonah's Gourd Vine:*

> What I wanted to tell was a story about a man, and from what I had read and heard, Negroes were supposed to write about the Race Problem. I was and am thoroughly

sick of the subject. My interest lies in what makes a man or a woman do such-and-such, regardless of his color.

To Hurston, her personality and wit were self-evident, and it was anyone's loss if they failed to see them. She said it best: "Sometimes I feel discriminated against, but it does not make me angry. It merely astonishes me. How can any deny themselves the pleasure of my company? It's beyond me."

CHAPTER SIX

LEGACY

The day after Hurston's death, Marjorie Silver, a local white reporter who had befriended her, received a phone call from the Percy S. Peek Funeral Home. She remembered: "They said they had Zora's body and didn't have enough to bury her and what should they do?" Silver did what she could: she wrote an article for the *Miami Herald* about Hurston's passing. Papers around the country, including the *New York Times* and *Time* magazine, soon picked up the article and began running their own obituaries. There were inconsistent reports of her age at the time of death that ranged from fifty-two to fifty-seven, though she was actually sixty-nine years old. However, the message was clear: she had died poor and without enough money for a $900 "proper" burial. Donations began pouring in from around the country, including from both her former publishers, Lippincott and Scribner's, as

Opposite: Hurston's hometown of Eatonville hosts the annual Zora! Festival in her honor. Here, artist Kolongi Bratiwaite attends the 2009 festival.

well as from Fannie Hurst, Carl Van Vechten, and schoolteachers and students from the high school Hurston once taught at. In the end, they raised $661.87, but the undertaker donated the burial plot, and the funeral was set for February 7, 1960.

Over one hundred people attended the services, including Hurston's family, community members, and sixteen white mourners. The funeral director, Curtis E. Johnson, recalled, "There were so many folks here we had to set chairs out to the sidewalk." The floral display was just as impressive: people from New York and all over the US had sent so many arrangements and wreathes that C. E. Bolan, owner of a local black paper in Fort Pierce, remarked, "you could hardly see the casket for the flowers." Silver remembered that Hurston was dressed in a "pale pink, fluffy something," and if she could see herself she "would have been holding her sides laughing." However, Hurston would have thoroughly enjoyed the rest: the local choir from the Lincoln Park Academy sang "Just a Closer Walk with Thee," and Baptists and Methodists, black and white folks, country and urban residents all came together to say goodbye to the woman who had touched their lives. The Reverend Wayman Jennings spoke eloquently about Hurston in his eulogy:

> Zora Neale went about and didn't care too much how she looked. Or what she said. Maybe people didn't think so much of that. But Zora Neale, everytime she went about, had something to offer. She didn't come to you empty. They said she couldn't become a writer recognized by the world. But she did it. The Miami paper said she died poor. But she died rich. She did something

Hurston was buried in the Garden of Heavenly Rest, Fort Pierce's segregated cemetery. The community collection did not raise enough money for a headstone, but her last physician, Dr. Benton, noted that Hurston "*didn't* have a pauper's funeral.

Everybody around here *loved* Zora." A few more words were said around the grave, and then Hurston was laid to rest.

As a young woman, Hurston may have prophesized her end, saying, "I am not materialistic … If I happen to die without money somebody will bury me though I do not wish it to be that way." Later in life, however, Hurston would remark on the end with a more spiritual approach: "I know that nothing is destructible: things merely change forms. When the consciousness we know as life ceases, I know that I shall still be part and parcel of the world."

Saving from the Fires

A few weeks after the funeral, Fannie Hurst wrote "Zora Neale Hurston: A Personality Sketch" for Yale University's *Library Gazette*. She described the late author as "a gift to both her race and the human race," and noted that any of her shortcomings, some of which she was privy to as her employer, were actually, "part of a charm you dared not douse." Hurst's final thoughts were:

> To life, to her people, she left a bequest of good writing and the memory of an iridescent personality of many colors. Her short shelf of writings deserves to endure. Undoubtedly, her memory will in the minds and hearts of her friends. We rejoice that she passed this way so brightly but alas, too briefly.

While Hurst was wrong in her assessment of Hurston's "short shelf of writing," she was right that her friends remembered her fondly. Carl Van Vechten wept when he read Hurst's words, saying:

> You make all the girl's faults seem to be her virtues. As a matter of fact, they were NOT faults, they were characteristics and there's quite a difference. What it comes down to is

Carl Van Vechten was one of Hurston's lifetime friends and artistic peers. He photographed many of Hurston's most famous portraits.

the fact that Zora was put together entirely different from the rest of mankind. Her reactions were always original because they were always her OWN.

While those in the North kept Hurston's memory alive, a strange turn of affairs in Florida almost literally burned her legacy to a cinder. One evening in February 1960, Patrick Duval, a black deputy at the St. Lucie County Sheriff's Department, was driving past Hurston's old home when he saw smoke rising from the backyard. He rushed to find that a group of men who had been hired to clear out the author's belongings were burning her storage trunk. Duval was aware of Hurston and knew that the trunk could be valuable, so thinking quickly, he grabbed a hose and put out the fire. Thanks to his fast actions, many of Hurston's papers were saved, including research and an incomplete manuscript of "The Life of Herod the Great."

Marjorie Silver was once again contacted to sort through the materials. In 1961, she donated the collection to the Department of Rare Books and Manuscripts at the University of Florida in Gainesville, as Hurston had intended. The collection would slowly grow over the years, and today the University of Florida's Smathers Libraries collection holds a room full of Hurston's correspondence, articles, manuscripts, photographs, and miscellaneous personal papers. The entire collection has been digitized and is available to search, a feat that would have been impossible had these materials not been saved for posterity.

RESURRECTION

Hurston had always been unconventional in her opinions and approach and was almost lost to time because of it. She did not fit into one movement, style, or career but transcended them all.

As a result, her name was often omitted from a renewed interest in black history in the early 1970s. The controversial "Harlem on My Mind" exhibition debuted at the Metropolitan Museum of Art in 1969 with photographs of many of Hurston's contemporaries such as Langston Hughes, Countee Cullen, Ethel Waters, and Billie Holiday. However, Hurston was nowhere to be found. The **Black Arts Movement (BAM)**, also controversial and short-lived, inspired many black creators to look back at generations past. Again, Hurston was overlooked. It seemed that only a decade after her death, her legacy was fading away.

Luckily, one author's renewed interest brought it back to life: Alice Walker. One of the most important authors of the twentieth century, Walker is a novelist, poet, social activist, and Pulitzer Prize winner. However, in 1973 she was just starting her career and looking to other black, female authors as examples. Much to her dismay, she found the list to be almost nonexistent. This was not because these figures did not exist, but because time had hidden them from the public eye. Walker wrote, "I became aware of my need of Zora Neale Hurston's work some time before I knew her work existed." Her first inclination was when she tried to research the folkways of African Americans in the 1930s. Walker looked for an authority on the subject so she could write a short story about it but came up empty handed. Later, when taking a class taught by a well-known black poet, she was disappointed to find only white, male authors populating the reading list. Barnard professor Monica Miller writes, "These two incidents taught Walker that to be a creative black woman ... was too often to be in a state of frustrating uniqueness or invisibility."

Walker knew there must be other African-American female writers out there, so she set out on a quest to discover her feminist and literary "foremothers." In 1983, Walker would publish these

Alice Walker, seen here at the Broadway opening of the musical version of her book *The Color Purple*, was instrumental in maintaining Hurston's legacy.

findings and thoughts as a collection of essays called *In Search of Our Mothers' Gardens*. She would coin the term **womanism**, a word that relates to a wide range of scholarship that supports women of color and their perspectives. Walker loosely defined a womanist as someone who "loves music. Loves dance. Loves the moon. Loves the Spirit. Loves love and food and roundness. Loves struggle. Loves the Folk. Loves herself. Regardless." She would soon discover that Zora Neale Hurston embodied these ideas herself.

Finding Hurston

Walker had heard Hurston's name mentioned in passing and in essay footnotes but knew little else about her. She had read as much of Hurston's work as she could—by this time all of Hurston's books had gone out of print—and knew that Eatonville held the key to her discovery. So on August 15, 1973, she flew to Florida to see what she could find. Charlotte Hunt, a white graduate student who was writing her dissertation on Hurston, picked Walker up at the airport. The two headed south, all the while Walker thinking: "Eatonville has lived for such a long time in my imagination that I can hardly believe it will be found existing in its own right."

However, they soon arrived at the real-life Eatonville. They headed to the city hall to ask if anyone in town had known Hurston. To avoid suspicion, Walker lied and said she was Hurston's niece. While the city clerk knew Hurston and had read her work, she noted that most of the town was unaware of her existence. She directed Walker and Hunt to Mrs. Moseley, an elderly but spunky woman who had gone to high school with Hurston. They learned that Joe Clarke's shop had become Club Eaton, a locally famous nightclub. Walker reflected how this was perhaps the modern version of the store's front porch. The most important thing Walker and Hunt learned was that Hurston had not been buried in Eatonville.

Next, they headed south to Fort Pierce and to the funeral parlor that had buried Hurston. Sarah Peek Patterson, the current owner, told them that her father had presided over Hurston's burial and he was too sick to speak to them. However, Patterson seemed to have a vague idea of where Hurston had been buried: "Just when you go in the gate there's a circle, and she's buried right in the middle of it. Hers is the only grave in that circle—because people don't bury in that cemetery anymore." She sent Walker, Hunt, and her own assistant, a young black woman named Rosalee, in the direction of the Garden of Heavenly Rest.

When they arrived, they realized the "circle" described covered over 1 acre (0.4 ha). Furthermore, the cemetery was unkempt, and the weeds were almost as tall as the women themselves. Walker and Rosalee plunged into the thicket, poking around, while Hunt stayed back. Walker called to her, asking, "Aren't you coming?" but she replied, "No, I'm from these parts and I know what's out there." Walker knew enough to know what this meant: snakes. Feeling it was too late to turn back now, she felt around furiously. She began to call out to Hurston: "I hope you don't think I'm going to stand out here all day, with these snakes watching me and these ants having a field day. In fact, I'm going to call you just one or two more times!"

Hurston's spirit must have happily complied, because almost a moment later Walker stepped into a sunken rectangle, roughly the shape of a grave. She called to Rosalee to join her, who was at first reluctant, but then decided to help. Walker thanked her, saying Hurston thanked her too, and the woman grinned back saying, "Just as long as she don't try to tell me in person."

Their adventure had paid off: they found Hurston's grave and headed to the nearest monument company to have a headstone made. Walker's first inclination was to buy the store's finest model, a black obelisk monument called "Ebony Mist." However, her budget only allowed for a modest gray tablet. She had the words engraved:

ZORA NEALE HURSTON
"A GENIUS OF THE SOUTH"
1901 1960
NOVELIST, FOLKLORIST
ANTHROPOLOGIST

Now, Walker's mission was complete. Before heading home she decided to try to find the home Hurston had spent her last years living in, as well as to visit Hurston's friend and physician Dr. Benton. She learned that Hurston was beloved by everyone in town. Dr. Benton spoke highly of the woman he admired, saying she had been fiercely active right until her stroke. After leaving the doctor, they drove to Hurston's home, which was in bad shape and owned by a woman who was away due to her ailing health. They discovered a neighbor who spoke fondly of Hurston as well, describing how she was an avid gardener and had kept her home alive with flowers and vegetation. She also had lived her final days with a companion named Sport: a big brown and white dog.

Alice Walker would culminate this experience in an essay entitled "Looking for Zora," which she published in 1975 for *Ms. Magazine*, a feminist magazine where she worked as an editor. Walker finished her essay by meditating on the impact Hurston's fate, and rediscovery, had on her:

> It is only later, when the pain is not so direct a threat to one's own existence, that what was learned in that moment of comical lunacy is understood. Such moments rob us of both our youth and vanity. But perhaps they are also times when greater disciplines are born.

LEGACY ALIVE

Thanks to Alice Walker's journey, Hurston went from forgotten to revered almost overnight. Many other prominent black authors, like Maya Angelou and Toni Morrison, would cite Hurston's work as a source of inspiration. Much like the multifaceted ways of Hurston's life, her legacy in death would take many forms.

Books

Only two years later, in 1977, scholar Robert E. Hemenway produced the first comprehensive biography on Zora Neale Hurston, drawing from research found in the Florida University Archives. Since then, thousands of essays, articles, and books have been written about Hurston's personal life, work, and impact. In 2003, scholar Carla Kaplan published *Zora Neale Hurston: A Life in Letters*, the first collection of Hurston's rich correspondence throughout her life. The same year, author Valerie Boyd wrote *Wrapped in Rainbows: The Life of Zora Neale Hurston*. Published by Hurston's former publisher Scribner's, the book dove into fascinating details about Hurston's life that had never before been revealed.

In addition to the countless works written about Hurston, nine of her books were published posthumously. These include collections of her short stories, additional folklore materials, writings made while in the Federal Writers Project, essay compilations, and even her scripts (*Mule Bone* included). Her remarkable literary career has been documented in countless bibliographies, and today, many of her articles have been reprinted or digitized and are available to read online.

Theater

Though Hurston never experienced success in the theater during her lifetime, her dramatic work has enjoyed a renaissance on its own. In the 1980s, American playwright and director George C. Wolfe began what the *Los Angeles Times* called a "Zora Revival." In 1989, he won an Obie Award for his off-Broadway production of *Spunk*, an adaption of three stories by Zora Neale Hurston. He received critical praise from the *New Yorker,* the *New York Times,* and *Variety,*

HURSTON'S PALATE

Hurston's work has been examined from many literary, social, and political perspectives. However, it wasn't until January 19, 2015, that someone explored her work on a culinary level. Frederick Douglass Opie, professor of history and foodways at Babson College, has published numerous books on the intersection of food and black culture, including *Zora Neale Hurston on Florida Food: Recipes, Remedies and Simple Pleasures*. The book follows Hurston's family lineage and relation to food, and includes the many recipes and anecdotes Hurston collected in the South. From the everyday to the formal, Opie traces the cuisine's African, Carribean, and even Asian origins and their evolution into the twentieth century incarnations Hurston cooked. Hurston's written recipes and photographs are contextualized with Opie's historical insights, allowing the book to be read as both a narrative and cookbook. The recipes are enough to make a modern-day foodie drool: ginger pear preserves, peanut coconut bars, collard greens, and fried chicken. One chapter even covers the many food and herbal remedies employed to help with minor to serious ailments. *Zora Neale Hurston on Florida Food* emphasizes the cultural importance of food in the black community. As Hurston wrote, describing one of the many town feasts she attended, "Over and above being neighborly and giving aid, there is the food, the drunks and the fun of getting together."

and continued to stage the show to great success until 1991. The *New York Post* wrote:

> The show—three pre–World War II vignettes of African-American life filtered through Hurston's black, ornery and feminist sensibility—has class, wit and passion … This is a great show … another tantalizing taste of the no longer forgotten Zora Neale Hurston.

In January 2016, an adaptation called *Spunk and the Harlem Literati* was directed by Be Boyd and performed at the University of Central Florida in conjunction with the 2016 Zora! Festival. Today this script is widely available and is performed by hundreds of troupes around the country.

Nearly sixty years after it was written, *Mule Bone* was finally staged for audiences at Lincoln Center, New York, in 1991. Directed by Michael Schultz, the performance received less than stellar reviews. The *New York Times* wrote a scathing review of the play but did point out its enduring legacy: "It's almost as if this maiden production were determined to make 'Mule Bone' prove on stage what it has always been in literary legend—a false start that remains one of the American theater's more tantalizing might-have-beens."

Not surprisingly, Hurston's vivid life and personality have also taken center stage. In 1986, Ellen Sebastian and Marilyn Waterman directed and co-wrote *The Sanctified Church*, a play based on Hurston's life and work, for the Life on the Water Theater in San Francisco. The production was then revised and renamed *Sanctified*, to be performed again in Los Angeles in 1990. *Letters from Zora* by Gabrielle Denise Pina is a play in two acts that "consists of authentic letters from Zora Neale Hurston fused with fictional narrative intended to illuminate her life, her extraordinary career and her contributions to the American literary canon." Opening for the DC Black Theater Festival in June 2015, the playwright was nominated for the NAACP Best Playwright Award, and the lead actress, who played Hurston herself, won the NAACP award for leading lady.

Florida's Native Daughter

The state of Florida has worked hard to reclaim its native daughter. Hurston's grave is no longer an unattended plot in the weeds but a well-manicured monument. The spot is even highlighted on the Fort Pierce "Zora Neale Hurston Dust Tracks Heritage Trail," which commemorates the life of the author with three large kiosks, eight trail markers, and an exhibition and visitors center. Additionally, Hurston's Fort Pierce home has now been added to the registry of national landmarks.

Eatonville, too, has continued to celebrate Hurston's legacy. The Zora Neale Hurston Museum of Fine Arts, also know as the Hurston, is a small visual art museum that highlights the works of artists of African descent. Eatonville is also home to the Zora! Festival, an annual celebration aimed at sustaining the local culture and honoring the legacy of its most famous resident. The 2016 festival was nine days long, with a host of events that ranged from serious scholarship to family fun.

Media

Hurston's life and works have even been adapted for different media. On January 7, 2014, Google created an illustrated "Google doodle" to celebrate Hurston's 123rd birthday. The image was a lovely portrait in an oval frame, decorated with folk-looking patterns, over a Florida marsh background. In 2005, Oprah Winfrey's Harpo Productions produced a film version of *Their Eyes Were Watching God* starring actress Halle Berry. Hurston herself has been the subject of numerous documentaries and has appeared as a character in various films about the Harlem Renaissance.

Literary Icon

In addition to the numerous awards and foundations Hurston was a part of in her own lifetime, she was posthumously inducted into the New York State Writers Hall of Fame in 2010 and the Alabama Writers Hall of Fame in 2015. In 2002, renowned scholar Molefi Kete Asante listed Hurston as one of the one hundred greatest African Americans, and in 2003, Barnard College dedicated the Virginia C. Gildersleeve Conference to Hurston under the title: "Jumpin at the Sun: Reassessing the Life and Work of Zora Neale Hurston."

Most of all, Hurston is and will continue to be known as a literary and scholarly icon. In addition to her fiction, Hurston provided a wealth of knowledge about African-American folklore and black lives in the early twentieth century. Her great storytelling ability wove beautiful, human tales that transcended their historical settings. Lastly, Zora Neale Hurston's life as a black woman in the early twentieth century is a testament to individuality and creativity, affirming that the life lived fully, and by one's own design, is the only life worth living.

1891 Zora Neale Hurston is born in Notasulga, Alabama.

1917 Hurston attends Morgan University in Baltimore.

1918 She moves to Washinton, DC, and attends Howard University.

1921 Publishes her first story, "John Redding Goes to Sea."

1924 Hurston wins the *Opportunity* contest for her story "Drenched in Light" and starts attending awards dinners in New York City.

1925 Receives a scholarship to be the first black woman to attend Barnard College.

1926 Hurston publishes *Fire!!* with Langston Hughes and other Harlem Rennaissance artists.

1927 Hurston makes her first unsuccessful trip to the South to collect folklore. She marries Herbert Sheen and signs a contract with Charlotte Osgood Mason.

1928 Hurston travels to Eatonville, Polk County, and New Orleans, graduates from Barnard, and publishes "How It Feels to Be Colored Me."

1929 Hurston travels to the Bahamas and lives through a hurricane.

1931 Her friendship and collaboration ends with Langston Hughes over *Mule Bone*; Hurston divorces Sheen.

1932 *The Great Day* is performed, and Hurston cuts ties with patron Charlotte Mason.

1935 Columbia University revokes her scholarship, and Hurston falls in love with Percy Punter.

1936 Awarded a Guggenheim grant, Hurston travels to Jamaica and Haiti.

1937 Hurston returns to Haiti on a renewed grant and publishes *Their Eyes Were Watching God*.

1948 Hurston is taken to court on molestation charges; *Seraph on the Suwanee* is published.

1952 Hurston is hired by *Pittsburg Courier* to write on Ruby McCollum case.

1959 Hurston suffers a stroke and is forced to go into a nursing home.

1960 Zora Neale Hurston dies of hypertensive heart disease and is buried in an unmarked grave in Fort Pierce, Florida.

HURSTON'S MOST IMPORTANT WORKS

SHORT STORIES

"John Redding Goes to Sea" (1921)
"Drenched in Light" (1924)
"Sweat" (1926)
"Gilded Six-Bits" (1933)

ESSAYS

"How It Feels to Be Colored Me" (1928)
"Hoodoo in America" (1931)
"What White Publishers Won't Publish" (1950)

THEATER

Color Struck (1925)
Mule Bone: A Comedy of Negro Life (1932)

NONFICTION BOOKS

Mules and Men (1935)
Tell My Horse (1938)
Dust Tracks on a Road (1942)

NOVELS

Jonah's Gourd Vine (1934)
Their Eyes Were Watching God (1937)
Moses, Man of the Mountain (1939)
Seraph on the Suwanne (1948)

African diaspora Referring to communities descended from the historic movement of African people during the slave trade.

allegories Stories or other creative works that can be evaluated to reveal a hidden political or cultural meaning.

anthropology The study of human cultures and how they develop.

anthropomorphic Endowing an animal or inanimate object with human qualities.

archetype The original pattern or model from which all things of the same kind are copied or on which they are based. A prototype or perfect example.

asceticism The act of imposing severe self-discipline and abstaining from indulgence, often for religious purposes.

Black Arts Movement (BAM) A controversial and short-lived art movement in the wake of Malcom X's assassination.

bootlegger A person who illegally makes or sells alcohol.

Brown v. Board of Education of Topeka, Kansas The landmark Supreme Court case that ruled segregation illegal.

classism Prejudice based on one's social standing.

cultural relativism The method to understand and study a culture by viewing it through that culture's own lens.

diasporic community A group of people who moved from their original place of birth, or ancestral home.

diatribe A bitter, sharply abusive denunciation, attack, or criticism.

empirical Guided by information gained through observation or experience.

ethnocentricity The belief that one's own culture is inherently superior to another by nature.

ethnography The scientific description of customs of a culture of people.

Eurocentric The belief that European culture and political systems are better than other cultures and political systems.

eye dialect The purposeful misspelling of words to imply the sound, pronunciation, and cadence of a character's speech.

fodder Material.

genteel Overly polite.

Harlem Renaissance A creative and social movement that took place in the neighborhood of Harlem, New York. Known at the time as the New Negro Movement.

idyllic Extremely happy, beautiful, or picturesque.

ingratiatingly Deliberately agreeable in an effort to gain favor.

Jim Crow laws Federal and state laws that enforced segregation.

Negrotarian A term used by Hurston to describe white liberals who financially or culturally supported black artists.

participatory research Research gleaned from a partnership with the community being studied.

primary source The original artifact for a source of information being studied.

provincialism The way of life in areas outside of big cities, often thought of as unsophisticated.

Reconstruction The time period following the Civil War during which the federal government sought to rebuild and unify the United States.

reflexivity Refers to two anthropological concepts: the first refers to the researcher's awareness of their relationship to the subject matter, and the second to the subject's self-reflection on his or her own culture.

revue A form of entertainment made up of skits, dances, and songs.

roman à clef French for "novel with a key," it refers to a novel that is based on real life but overlaid with fictional elements. The "key" is the relationship of reality to fiction: a layer of meaning lies between what has been changed and why.

rugged individualism A term coined by President Herbert Hoover during the onset of the Great Depression that refers to the idea that an individual should be able to pull him or herself up from poverty without assistance, and specifically without government assistance.

superstition A collective belief or notion, not based on reason or knowledge.

sympathetic magic Ritualistic magic that uses symbolic objects or actions to exercise influence over a person or event.

womanism A word that relates to a wide range of beliefs that support women of color and their perspectives.

Works Progress Administration (WPA) The federal program that employed Americans to work on public projects during the Great Depression.

BOOKS

Boyd, Valerie. *Wrapped in Rainbows: The Life of Zora Neale Hurston.* New York: Scribner, 2003.

Hemenway, Robert E. *Zora Neale Hurston: A Literary Biography.* Urbana: University of Illinois Press, 1977.

Jones, Sharon L. *Critical Companion to Zora Neale Hurston: A Literary Reference to Her Life and Work.* New York: Facts On File, 2009.

Kaplan, Carla, ed. *Zora Neale Hurston: A Life in Letters.* New York: Doubleday, 2002

Opie, Frederick Douglass. *Zora Neale Hurston on Florida Food: Recipes, Remedies and Simple Pleasures.* Charleston, SC: History Press, 2015.

WEBSITES

Lore Podcast, Episode 26: Brought Back
www.lorepodcast.com/episodes/26
This popular podcast is about Haitian zombies and includes a reading of Hurston's work.

Zora! Festival
zorafestival.org
This website includes information about the annual festival celebrating Hurston's life and work in Eatonville.

Zora Neale Hurston Digital Archive
chdr.cah.ucf.edu/hurstonarchive/?p=_home
The University of Central Florida's research archive has lots of valuable information about Zora Neale Hurston.

"About Zora Neale Hurston." The Official Website of Zora Neale Hurston. Accessed February 15, 2016. http://zoranealehurston.com/about.

"A Guide to the Zora Neale Hurston Papers." University of Florida Smathers Libraries, August 2008. Accessed February 15, 2016. http://www.uflib.ufl.edu/spec/manuscript/hurston/hurston.htm.

"Alice Walker Shines Light on Zora Neale Hurston." PBS, 2014. American Masters Series. http://www.pbs.org/video/2365167356.

"Archaeology of a Classic: Celebrating Zora Neale Hurston '28.". Barnard University, December 17, 2012. Accessed February 15, 2016. http://barnard.edu/news/archaeology-classic-celebrating-zora-neale-hurston-28.

Boyd, Valerie. "Wrapped in Rainbows." Valerie Boyd - Writer - Editor - Educator. Accessed February 15, 2016. http://www.valerieboyd.com/wrapped-in-rainbows.

———. *Wrapped in Rainbows: The Life of Zora Neale Hurston*. New York: Scribner, 2003.

Clifford, Sean. "African-American and Creole Traditions Surrounding Death in the Cane River Region." National Center for Preservation Training and Technology. September 22, 2011. Accessed February 15, 2016. https://ncptt.nps.gov/blog/african-american-and-creole-traditions-surrounding-death-in-the-cane-river-region.

"The Coming of a Town." Eatonville History. 2011. Accessed February 15, 2016. https://eatonvillefl.wordpress.com/history.

"Documents on Zora Neale Hurston from the Barnard College Archives." Barnard Center for Research on Women. Accessed February 15, 2016. http://sfonline.barnard.edu/hurston/archives_01.htm.

DuCille, Ann. "Looking for Zora." *New York Times*, January 5, 2003.

Egbert, Connor, Jack Elliot, and Matthew Franks. "The Historical Town of Eatonville, Florida." Their Eyes Were Watching God PD 4, December 16, 2013. Accessed February 15, 2016. http://blakefield.typepad.com/advancedlitatblakefield4/2013/12/the-historical-town-of-eatonville-florida.html.

Gates, Henry Louis, Jr. "THEATER; Why the 'Mule Bone' Debate Goes On." *New York Times*, February 10, 1991. Accessed February 15, 2016. http://www.nytimes.com/1991/02/10/theater/theater-why-the-mule-bone-debate-goes-on.html?pagewanted=all.

"Google Doodle: Zora Neale Hurston's 123rd Birthday." Digital image. Google Doodle Archive, January 7, 2014. Accessed February 15, 2016. http://www.google.com/doodles/zora-neale-hurstons-123rd-birthday.

Graham, Adam H. "Forgotten Florida, Through a Writer's Eyes." *New York Times*, March 31, 2010. Accessed February 15, 2016. http://www.nytimes.com/2010/04/04/travel/04culture.html?_r=0.

"Guide—Zora Neale Hurston: 1891–1960." Howard University Library System. Accessed February 15, 2016. http://www.howard.edu/library/reference/guides/hurston.

Harrison, J. L. "On the Impossibility of True Intellectual Assimilation." Accessed February 15, 2016. http://userpages.umbc.edu/~jamie/html/on_the_impossibility_of_true_i.html.

Hemenway, Robert E. *Zora Neale Hurston: A Literary Biography.* Urbana: University of Illinois Press, 1977.

"The History of Florida Turpentine Camps." Herald-Tribune, March 15, 2004. Accessed February 15, 2016. http://www.heraldtribune.com/article/20040315/NEWS/403150625.

Holland, Norwood. "Hurston and Hurst: Setting the Record Straight." *Norwood Holland's Editorial Independence.* November 10, 2011. Accessed February 15, 2016. http://www.editorialindependence.com/2011/11/10/hurston-and-hurst-setting-the-record-straight.

Hurston, Zora Neale. *Dust Tracks on a Road: An Autobiography.* Urbana: University of Illinois Press, 1984.

———. "How It Feels to Be Colored Me." 1928.

———. *Mules and Men.* New York: Perennial Library, 1990.

———. *Sweat.* Edited by Cheryl A. Wall. New Brunswick, NJ: Rutgers University Press, 1997.

———. *Tell My Horse: Voodoo and Life in Haiti and Jamaica.* Edited by Henry Louis Gates Jr. New York: Harper Perennial, 2009.

———. *The Complete Stories.* New York: HarperCollins, 1995.

———. *Their Eyes Were Watching God: A Novel.* New York: Perennial Library, 1990.

———. "What White Publishers Won't Print." Negro Digest, April 1950.

———. Zora Neale Hurston: A Life in Letters. Edited by Carla Kaplan. New York: Doubleday, 2002.

JoAnn. "Short Story Monday: 'The Eatonville Anthology' by Zora Neale Hurston." Lakeside Musing, February 22, 2010. Accessed February 15, 2016. http://lakesidemusing.blogspot.com/2010/02/short-story-monday-eatonville-anthology.html.

Jones, Sharon L. Critical Companion to Zora Neale Hurston: A Literary Reference to Her Life and Work. New York: Facts On File, 2009.

Jones, Sharon L., ed. Critical Insights: Zora Neale Hurston. Ipswich, MA: Salem Press, 2013.

Ladd, Barbara. Resisting History: Gender, Modernity, and Authorship in William Faulkner, Zora Neale Hurston, and Eudora Welty. Baton Rouge: Louisiana State University Press, 2007.

Locke, Alain. Opportunity 17 (1939): 38.

Mahnke, Aaron. "Episode 26: Brought Back." Lore Podcast, January 25, 2016. http://www.lorepodcast.com.

Martin, Ronald E. The Languages of Difference: American Writers and Anthropologists Reconfigure the Primitive, 1878–1940. Newark: University of Delaware Press, 2005.

McClaurin, Irma. "Zora Neale Hurston, The Making of an Anthropologist." Savage Minds: Notes and Queries in Anthropology, December 27, 2014. Accessed February 15, 2016. http://savageminds.org/2014/12/27/zora-neale-hurston-the-making-of-an-anthropologist.

Opie, Frederick Douglass. *Zora Neale Hurston on Florida Food: Recipes, Remedies and Simple Pleasures*. Charleston, SC: History Press, 2015.

Pardee, Shiela Ellen. "Rites as Role Playing in Zorah Neale Hurston's Tell My Horse." *Women Writers: A Zine*, August 2008. Accessed February 15, 2016. http://www.womenwriters.net/aug08/HurstonPardee.htm.

Peters, Pearlie Mae Fisher. *The Assertive Woman in Zora Neale Hurston's Fiction, Folklore, and Drama*. New York: Garland Pub., 1998.

"Play Inspiration." Letters from Zora. Accessed February 15, 2016. http://lettersfromzora.com/play-inspiration.html.

Rayson, Ann L. "Dust Tracks on a Road: Zora Neale Hurston on the Form of Black Autobiography." *Negro American Literature Forum* 7, no. 2 (Summer 1973): 39-45.

Rich, Frank. "Review/Theater; A Difficult Birth For 'Mule Bone'" *New York Times*, February 15, 1991. Accessed February 15, 2016. http://www.nytimes.com/1991/02/15/theater/review-theater-a-difficult-birth-for-mule-bone.html?pagewanted=all.

Sebastian, Ellen. "STAGE: Reclaiming Zora's Spirit." Los *Angeles Times*, September 15, 1991. http://articles.latimes.com/1991-09-15/entertainment/ca-3723_1_stories-by-harlem-renaissance-zora-neale-hurston-spunk.

Walker, Alice. *In Search of Our Mothers' Gardens: Womanist Prose*. San Diego, CA: Harcourt Brace Jovanovich, 1983.

————. "Looking for Zora." In *I Love Myself When I Am Laughing and Then Again When I Am Looking Mean and Impressive*, edited by Alice Walker. New York: The Feminist Press, 1979.

Watson, Steven. *The Harlem Renaissance: Hub of African-American Culture, 1920-1930*. New York: Pantheon Books, 1995.

Wright, Richard. "Between Laughter and Tears." New Masses, October 5, 1937.

Yates, Janelle, and David Adams. *Zora Neale Hurston: A Storyteller's Life*. Staten Island, NY: Ward Hill Press, 1991.

"Zora Neale Hurston." Bio.com. Accessed February 15, 2016. http://www.biography.com/people/zora-neale-hurston 9347659#synopsis.

"Zora Neale Hurston Digital Archive." Zora Neale Hurston Digital Archive. Accessed February 15, 2016. http://chdr.cah. ucf.edu/hurstonarchive/?p=_home.

INDEX

Page numbers in **boldface** are illustrations. Entries in **boldface** are glossary terms.

Lara Antal is a born-and-raised Wisconsinite. She writes about art to understand it. She makes her own art to understand everything else.